PRAISE FOR *SO YOU GOT THE PRIVACY OFFICER TITLE. NOW WHAT?*

"A straightforward, realistic, and encouraging guide to privacy work, regardless of what career stage you are at. The author repeatedly emphasizes that privacy practice requires a cross-functional and flexible skill set. This book identifies both the obvious and the less apparent skills, then provides easy-to-execute strategies for success. It uses real-world scenarios to emphasize points and keep you engaged. As an attorney changing tracks mid-career, this book gave me the confidence to know which of my existing skills are most valuable and what areas still need developing."
— **Kavita Gupta,** Recently Certified Privacy Professional

"The single most frequent request I received as a regulator was for the provision of more practical, real-world guidance and case studies to support best-practice data protection and privacy implementation on the ground. Teresa Troester-Falk has downloaded and distilled her own extensive career delivering global privacy programmes into the most valuable, truly operational guidebooks that will fast-track any privacy professional, across any jurisdiction, to outcomes that are more than "good enough." In an EU context, the GDPR requires the Data Protection Officer not just to have expert knowledge but also the necessary "professional qualities"—Teresa nails the coaching of those essential qualities."
—**Helen Dixon,** Former Data Protection Commissioner for Ireland

"Teresa has managed to distill the practical takeaways from decades of experience into a guide that provides the real-world know-how privacy professionals need. Learning data protection law is the easiest part; learning how to build a program in an uncertain and changing environment takes years of trial and error and struggle. Teresa shares the invaluable hard-won lessons from her career and from colleagues in the community that will be invaluable to anyone working in data protection or artificial intelligence."
—**Jules Polonetsky,** CEO, Future of Privacy Forum, Former CPO AOL and DoubleClick

"This practical guide is a 'must-have' for the privacy professional in your life! Teresa has distilled years of experience working with privacy teams into a concise toolkit for how to handle the most important privacy challenges practically, efficiently, and in a prioritized way that best supports the business. This book meets the privacy challenges of today—AI, privacy impact assessments, vendor risk management, understanding your data—with pragmatic guidance that will help both those new to a privacy leadership role and experienced privacy professionals! As a many-time privacy officer, this would have been on my bookshelf!"
—**Sharon A. Anolik,** President, Privacy Panacea LLC

"Teresa has been an incredible mentor to me, and her *So You Got The Privacy Officer Title. Now What?* book reflects why. It's a rare and invaluable guide for privacy professionals navigating real-world challenges. Its practical examples, grounded advice, and operational insights would have saved me countless hours and missteps when building my first program. Even now, it's an essential reference for continuous improvement, helping me translate theory into action with confidence. Whether you're new to privacy or seeking fresh perspectives on implementation, this book provides clear, actionable guidance that bridges the gap between what you're taught in certifications and meaningful, sustainable practices."
—**Alexys Carlton,** Principal, Privacy & AI Governance Analyst, iCIMS

SO YOU GOT THE PRIVACY OFFICER TITLE.

NOW WHAT?

Building a Privacy Program Without Budget, Authority, or a Clear Plan

Teresa “T” Troester-Falk

Published by BlueSky PrivacyStack.
Paperback: 979-8-9931121-0-7
Hardcover: 979-8-9931121-1-4

Disclaimer:
This book is intended for educational and informational purposes only. It does not constitute legal advice, nor does it create an attorney-client relationship. The author and publisher make no representations or warranties about the accuracy or applicability of the content in any specific situation. Readers are advised to consult a qualified attorney or privacy professional for advice tailored to their individual circumstances.

"Teresa is one of the GOATs in the privacy industry. Her "been there" and "done that" spans not only time but also legal frameworks, industries, privacy technology, and continents. In this book, Teresa gives us her hard-earned insights into operationalizing privacy and explains it in easy-to-understand terms. Using step-by-step instructions, she describes how to create a privacy program you can explain, maintain, and defend. Excellent!!"
—**Janelle Hsia,** President, Privacy SWAN Consulting, and Founder and VP, Institute of Operational Privacy Design

"As a longtime People & Culture leader in data-driven companies, and then CEO of a business supporting startups across many industries, I've seen firsthand how hard it is to build effective programs with limited resources and to communicate risk to leadership. This book delivers what privacy teams need most: judgment over checklists, plain-spoken playbooks, and the 'influence without authority' skills that earn trust in the boardroom."
—**Cathy Hawley,** Leadership Consultant, Former Chief People Officer, COO and CEO

"This book is the resource I wish I had when I first stepped into a privacy role. It goes beyond theory and certifications to show how privacy actually gets done inside organizations—with real constraints, competing priorities, and limited authority. This book offers strategies that are as valuable to a senior privacy counsel as they are to someone stepping into the role for the first time. It delivers immediate value and clear guidance to anyone navigating the realities of building a privacy program under pressure."
—**Mike Harrigan,** Senior Counsel, Privacy and Technology - Wrangler & Lee

"This is a cheat sheet for building an effective privacy program without having to endure the pain of learning from mistakes. Teresa's understanding and experience are second to none, and this shines through in this book. Many books on this topic confuse rather than elucidate; this one is the exception—clear, concise, and practical. Essential reading for budding privacy professionals."
—**Dr. John Ghent,** CEO & Co-founder, PrivacyEngine

DEDICATION

To my sons:

Ben – Your clarity, profound curiosity, and grounded nature have been a quiet strength in my life. Your gentle way of seeing the world keeps stretching mine.

Jesse– You've changed me in ways words can't hold. The path you walk continues to widen my sense of love, connection, and all that's possible.

TABLE OF CONTENTS

INTRODUCTION

So You Know Privacy Law. Now What?

Maybe you passed your privacy certification last month or you've been doing this work for years. You know the definitions, privacy frameworks, the lawful bases. But when you're at work, reality hits. *"Can we share this list with our partners?" "Marketing wants to launch something new. Can I approve it?" "This data subject request. Is it even valid?"* It feels like you're fighting the same battles over and over.

You don't need more theory. You need clarity when the Slack messages start piling up and the business is moving faster than your to-do list.

This book is here to meet that moment. It's written for the privacy professional committed to doing this work well, often without clear support or structure. Whether you're the only person thinking about privacy in your organization or you're part of a team still figuring out what ownership looks like, the insights in this book are meant to help you move forward with confidence.

You'll find approaches for navigating complexity and pressure. Not abstract frameworks, but grounded practices that have proven to work in context.

What This Book Is (and Isn't)

This book does not constitute legal advice.

It focuses on the operational middle ground where privacy gets implemented. This is the space between legal requirements and technical solutions where most privacy work happens. Whether you come from legal, business, or technical backgrounds, you'll discover approaches for navigating the organizational dynamics, stakeholder relationships, and practical judgment calls that determine whether privacy initiatives succeed or fail.

You may not agree with every approach, and that's expected. Ask ten privacy professionals how to handle the same request and you'll get ten different, often valid, answers! This book is part of that evolving conversation.

> Use what's useful. Adapt what isn't. Share your own version. That's how this field gets stronger: through transparency, iteration, and mutual support.

I've focused on operational foundations for structuring a privacy program that you can explain, maintain, and defend.

You won't find coverage of specialized areas like data breach incident response (typically managed by IT Security and Legal), complex international data transfer mechanisms, or advanced privacy engineering (areas that require specific legal counsel or technical expertise). What you will find here are practical tools and insights to help you build or refresh a privacy compliance infrastructure.

Who This Book Is For

This book is for privacy professionals who need practical guidance, whether you're new to the field, leading a small team, or transitioning from legal or IT or other departments. You might have a new CIPP certification, but are unsure how to apply that knowledge. You might be working alone in a mid-size company or part of a fast-paced team trying to understand how privacy works in practice.

It's also for experienced professionals seeking a fresh perspective on operational fundamentals. This includes those shifting from legal work to hands-on implementation, moving from structured organizations to leaner ones, or building a more proactive approach after years of reactive problem-solving.

It does not cover large-scale multinational programs or complex enterprise frameworks. Instead, whether you're building a program, working to influence others without formal authority, or simply looking for tools that work in real-world settings, this book helps you move from asking "What now?" to saying "I can handle this," with confidence to manage core privacy tasks and escalate issues when needed.

Why I Wrote This Book

Because I have been there.

I have carried privacy programs in environments that moved fast and did not always value the work. I have navigated the tension between risk and speed, between good intentions and unclear ownership. I have spent long hours translating legal theory into something people could actually use, and I know you have too.

The clarity I have gained did not come from theory. It came from the people I have worked alongside–practical, sharp, deeply committed professionals who helped shape better answers and pressure-test ideas. Their thinking runs through every page of this book.

The insight in this book also came from the broader privacy community. The ones troubleshooting in real time, swapping templates and half-finished drafts, figuring things out together across Slack threads, Zoom calls, and conference side chats. I would not have made it through the hardest moments in this field without that network of fellow professionals, many of whom I now count as friends.

> As automation continues to expand, what matters most is the work it cannot replace: sound judgment, practical insight, and steady leadership.

Leading privacy technology providers are starting to acknowledge this. Their most successful customers are not the ones chasing the most features. They are the ones who build clear, grounded programs, who understand their data, define ownership, and make sound decisions before introducing automation. The best platforms do not create order, they scale it.

At its core, privacy is personal. It is about taking responsibility for how people's information is used. It is about showing up with clarity, accountability, and care. Much of it is unglamorous work that must be done well.

If you are doing that work, often quietly and under pressure, this book is for you.

What follows is practical. It is not perfect, and it is not final. Let it be a starting point; something you can build on, adapt, and make your own.

You are not behind. You are exactly where you need to be.

No One Builds a Working Privacy Program Alone.
The best ones are built through collaboration, improvisation, and shared wisdom. This book is one voice in that ongoing conversation. Yours belongs in it too.

PART I:

MAKING PRIVACY WORK

Every privacy professional remembers the moment when the textbook knowledge stops being enough. Certification teaches concepts, frameworks, and legal requirements. It gives you vocabulary and structure. But stepping into a real privacy role reveals something different: organizations don't operate like exam questions, and business leaders rarely wait for perfect answers.

This part of the book is about that first critical shift: from theory to practice. It's where knowledge meets the friction of real organizations, competing priorities, incomplete information, and constant time pressure. The gap between what you've studied and what the role demands can feel jarring, even disorienting. But it's not a sign of failure. It's the natural next stage of growth for every privacy professional.

In the chapters ahead, we'll explore the challenges that define these early months: moving past perfection paralysis, learning how to translate legal language into business action, finding influence when you lack formal authority, and building confidence in your own judgment. You'll see how privacy becomes less about reciting the rules and more about making workable decisions in gray areas – decisions that can stand up to scrutiny while still allowing the business to move forward.

This part sets the foundation for everything else in this book. It helps you recognize the predictable obstacles you will encounter, reframe them as opportunities to build credibility, and start developing the judgment that separates strong privacy leaders from those who never move beyond compliance checklists.

CHAPTER 1:

THE GAP BETWEEN CERTIFICATION AND IMPLEMENTATION

Beyond "Now You Know Privacy"

You've studied the principles. You know the frameworks. You're familiar with the lawful bases. The regulatory requirements. And now you're in a real-world role where someone needs to be the go-to person for privacy in your organization.

So... why does everything still feel like uncharted territory?

Understanding privacy law is only the foundation. The real challenge is putting those principles into practice when business needs, technical constraints, and regulatory demands all come into play.

Many privacy professionals experience a confidence crisis during their first months in their role. The gap between what certification taught and what daily practice requires feels like personal inadequacy rather than the predictable transition that it actually is. Certification provided essential knowledge. But the skills that matter most, like judgment, stakeholder management, and practical risk assessment, can only be developed through real-world experience that no textbook can replicate.

Learning to work through this challenge while building the systems and relationships that make privacy sustainable becomes essential to your long-term success.

When Theory Meets Reality

One week into a new privacy role, you're staring at a vendor's Data Processing Agreement that uses completely different terminology than your certification materials. Marketing needs an answer by Friday because they've already committed to a launch date. What should have been a "quick review" stretches into hours of questioning what you actually know. The contract isn't obviously wrong: it just isn't right either. Is this an acceptable risk or a compliance red flag? The business is waiting for your expert opinion, but expertise feels distant.

Two weeks later, you receive a data subject request for "all my information" from someone who provided only an email address. The legal deadline is approaching, but the organization has no inventory of where customer data lives. Certification covered access rights thoroughly, but not the operational complexity of actually fulfilling them.

A month in, marketing launches a campaign that technically violates the privacy notice. Nobody noticed until a customer complained. Do you stop the campaign mid-flight? Update the notice retroactively?

These scenarios reveal the fundamental challenge: the transition from theoretical knowledge to practical judgment.

Knowledge vs. Judgment: The Critical Distinction

Most privacy education focuses on the *what* and *why*: what regulations require, why privacy matters, what programs should include. Day-to-day privacy work, on the other hand, centers on the *when* and *how*: when to push back versus when to find workable compromises, how to get buy-in without authority, when perfect compliance isn't realistic.

Knowledge encompasses frameworks learned through training: legal requirements, regulatory guidance, best practices. It's comprehensive and usually testable.

Judgment develops through experience: knowing which risks translate to practical compliance gaps, when to adapt processes for business reality, how to time interventions for maximum impact. It's contextual, nuanced and constantly evolving.

The difference becomes clear in practice. Knowledge tells you what an ideal data processing agreement should contain. Judgment helps you assess whether this particular agreement creates meaningful risk or merely theoretical imperfection, and how to prioritize limited negotiating capital based on actual data flows and vendor risk levels.

The Four Walls Most Privacy Professionals Hit

The transition from certification to implementation reveals predictable challenges that catch people unprepared, regardless of their technical background or regulatory knowledge.

The Perfection Paralysis

Privacy training focuses on theoretical completeness, but real organizations require pragmatic solutions. Waiting for perfect information can mean that nothing gets implemented: decisions get made without privacy input.

The Translation Challenge

Certification teaches communication among privacy professionals, but the reality is that most stakeholders aren't privacy professionals. Saying a practice "violates Article 25" doesn't help a product manager understand what needs to change.

The Authority Paradox

You're responsible for organizational compliance without authority to enforce requirements. You can't personally review every campaign or contract. The role evolves from solving individual problems to building organizational competence.

The Confidence Crisis

When business leaders expect definitive answers, admitting uncertainty feels like failure. The fear of making wrong decisions leads to paralysis just when decisive guidance is needed most. Privacy expertise isn't about having perfect knowledge of every scenario. It's about developing sound judgment and the confidence to apply it.

The Path Forward

Certification provides the essential foundation of knowledge. It enables everything that follows, but it's only the beginning.

This book addresses the foundational areas where practical judgment develops:

Working with concrete problems rather than perfect frameworks. The most effective privacy professionals start by identifying something that's actually broken and fixing it, building credibility and understanding through visible progress.

Focusing on outcomes rather than activities. Success isn't measured by policies written or training sessions conducted, but by whether teams understand the why and consistently follow through on privacy practices that are practical, meaningful, and built to last.

Building relationships across business functions. Privacy doesn't happen in isolation. Marketing teams face campaign deadlines, product managers work within technical constraints, sales teams respond to customer requirements. Effective privacy guidance acknowledges these competing priorities.

Developing comfort with "good enough" solutions. Most privacy decisions involve trade-offs between competing priorities. The skill lies in making defensible decisions with incomplete information and improving over time.

In the following chapters, we will focus on building operational capabilities through practical application. You know what privacy laws require. Now we'll learn how to make those requirements work in real organizations, with real constraints, serving real people.

CHAPTER 2:

UNDERSTANDING ORGANIZATIONS AND BUILDING INFLUENCE

The Reality No Certification Prepares You For

You won't always have executive buy-in, but the work still has to be done.

Privacy depends on coordination across the business, but that doesn't mean you'll always have authority, budget, or visibility, especially at the start. You might be working solo, with little more than a title and a vague mandate to "make us compliant."

And yet, expectations are high. You're expected to reduce risk, respond to requests, manage vendors, and approve marketing initiatives, often without the influence to make privacy a priority.

The disconnect between responsibility and authority is jarring, but it's also normal. You don't need full alignment on day one. You need a foothold and a clear, confident way to start.

The Org Chart Can Be Misleading

Mature privacy requires structure: clear ownership, aligned priorities, formalized controls, and scalable processes. But getting there is a long process that does not happen overnight. As you address the most important privacy compliance initiatives, you may find that the org chart isn't always helpful. You think you need to go to Legal, Security, or IT to "get privacy done," but here's what you may actually find:

- ☞ **Legal** cares about risk, not implementation
- ☞ **Security** cares about threats, not privacy rights
- ☞ **IT** cares about uptime and budget, not deletion workflows
- ☞ **Marketing** mostly cares that you don't kill their funnels

Who actually can help you get some of the critical privacy compliance work done? People who aren't on your radar yet: a project manager who controls the product roadmap, an IT lead who built a shadow system five years ago and never told Legal, a finance analyst who knows which vendors actually get paid.

Until your program develops maturity and strong executive support, the effective, operational work often happens through relationships with people who have practical influence, not formal authority.

Finding the Network That Gets Things Done

You've probably experienced that most companies seem to have two organizational structures: the one on paper and the one that actually executes the work.

The **official network** shows reporting lines, budget authority, and formal approvals. It tells you who signs what and who gets invited to executive meetings.

The **working network** shows information flow, problem-solving relationships, and practical influence. It tells you who knows what's actually happening, who can make changes stick, and who other people go to when they need to solve problems.

For privacy work, the working network can be everything.

The Four Trails to Follow

→ **Follow the data.** Who actually handles customer information daily?

Often it's customer service reps, sales operations, or marketing analysts – not the people who designed the systems. These are the people who know where data actually lives, how it moves between systems, and what happens when processes break down. They're also the ones who can tell you about the work-arounds that never made it into official documentation.

→ **Follow the problems.** When something breaks, who gets called?

These are your real system owners, regardless of what the org chart says. They're the people who understand how things actually work because they're the ones who have to fix them. They also tend to be pragmatic problem-solvers who appreciate solutions that make their lives easier.

→ **Follow the decisions.** Who do people ask when they're unsure?

These informal advisors often have more influence than formal managers. They're the people who've been around long enough to understand the context behind decisions, who know which battles are worth fighting, and who can help you navigate political dynamics.

→ **Follow the shortcuts.** When official processes don't work, who do people go to?

These relationship brokers can make or break your privacy initiatives. They know how to get things done when the formal process would take six months, and they're usually willing to help if you make it worth their while. These connectors aren't always high-ranking, but they often know how to get blockers removed fast.

Why Privacy Ownership Gets Complicated

This network mapping isn't just an academic exercise. Unlike cybersecurity (almost always IT's domain) or contracts (Legal's domain), privacy touches marketing, legal, product, HR, customer service, and operations. It cuts across almost all key departments.

No single department owns it naturally, which means that often everyone assumes someone else is handling it:

- Marketing assumes Legal reviewed the privacy implications
- Legal assumes IT implemented the technical controls
- IT assumes the business teams know what data they actually need

The Result: Data privacy becomes everyone's responsibility, which often means it's no one's responsibility.

One of your effective roles is to change that dynamic by building relationships with the people who can actually make things happen.

Building Effective Relationships Through Value Creation

Success starts with showing up prepared. It sounds simple, but it's actually difficult to implement when we have been steeped in the law and regulations. Below are effective methods that are tried and true.

Show Up Prepared

Generic discovery meetings rarely build credibility. You'll have much more success if you do your homework first. Preparation turns meetings into momentum.

Instead of: *"Can you tell me about your CRM setup?"*

Try: *"I see you're using HubSpot for lead management. I'm trying to understand if leads can opt out of specific email types. Can we walk through how preferences get set?"*

This shows you've done basic research and have a specific goal for the conversation.

Make Their Work Easier

The key is solving problems for key stakeholders, not creating new ones.

> **Field Insight:** When the analytics team was building new dashboards to track customer behavior, they were unsure which data fields were safe to use. Instead of slowing them down with a long policy document, we created a quick-reference data guide that flagged fields with consent requirements or sensitivity considerations. With this in hand, they moved faster, avoided compliance issues, and appreciated having clear, actionable guidance without the legal jargon.

Speak Their Language

Use their priorities as your privacy entry point. Instead of talking about legal requirements, try focusing on business outcomes they care about:

Function	What They Care About	Privacy Translation
Marketing	Lead generation, campaign performance	"This will reduce spam complaints and improve deliverability"
IT	System uptime, budget efficiency	"This eliminates a manual process and reduces security exposure"
Sales	Lead quality, conversion rates	"This helps us avoid prospects who'll likely never convert anyway"

The goal isn't to disguise privacy requirements as business benefits, but to find the genuine alignment between good privacy practices and business outcomes. When you can show how privacy compliance makes their work better, not just legally compliant, you build allies instead of creating obstacles.

Making Privacy Easier Than the Workaround

Most people don't have bad intentions when they bypass privacy controls. They're just busy and under pressure to meet their own deadlines or leadership goals.

Marketing lives in campaign cycles. Product teams are measured on shipping velocity. Sales teams have quotas. If privacy means more friction, most people will try to find ways around it.

That's not a personal attack on your work; it's an invitation to build effective and efficient privacy systems.

Build Into Existing Workflows

An effective approach is building privacy into existing workflows rather than creating parallel processes.

Don't: Require a separate privacy review for every vendor
Do: Add privacy questions to the existing vendor onboarding form

Don't: Ask teams to remember privacy requirements
Do: Work to set agreed-upon defaults that protect privacy automatically

Use Smart Defaults

Set new user profiles to minimum necessary visibility, not maximum. Design dashboards to hide sensitive fields unless specifically needed. Defaults shape behavior more effectively than policies.

Create Ready-to-Use Templates

Give people language they can use without thinking:

> **Template Example:** *"Hi Team, before we move forward with the new marketing integration, let's make sure we have proper permission to use the vendor and that they've been reviewed. Can you send over the vendor's privacy policy or platform ID? I'll loop in the web team to confirm our cookie banner and consent settings are covered."*

This approach acknowledges the reality that people will take the path of least resistance. And we best support the teams when we ensure that path is privacy-compliant.

Building Credibility Without Authority

You're not the Chief Privacy Officer. You're not a lawyer. You may not even have "privacy" in your title. None of that usually matters in practice.

Your credibility will come from:

- ☞ **Showing up prepared**
- ☞ **Offering real solutions instead of legal lectures**
- ☞ **Following through consistently and reliably**

Solve Problems Before People Ask

One of the most powerful things you can do is solve problems before people ask. Notice what's broken and fix it, then tell people what you fixed and why it matters.

> **Example:** While reviewing a privacy notice, you might test the listed contact email for data requests and discover it's unmonitored due to a misconfigured routing rule. Fix the issue, set up an internal alert system to flag incoming requests, then communicate what you did: *"This ensures we don't miss legal deadlines and improves trust with users."*

Provide Options, Not Ultimatums

When people come to you with requests, provide options instead of ultimatums.

Instead of: *"You can't do that"*
Try: *"Here are three ways to achieve your goal while managing privacy risk"*

Explain trade-offs clearly and help people understand the real consequences of different choices:

> *"Option A is faster but creates ongoing compliance work. Option B takes longer upfront but automates compliance. Option C splits the difference. What works best for your timeline?"*

This approach builds credibility because it shows you understand business needs and can think strategically about solutions. You're not just the person who says no. You will become the person who helps find a way to say yes while managing risk appropriately.

Working in the Gray Areas

You will not get perfect answers. You will be asked to approve things with unclear risk. You will have to make judgment calls, sometimes fast. You'll be interpreting policies that don't match reality, documenting processes you don't control, and negotiating between user rights and business goals.

That's privacy in practice. If you're waiting for someone to give you permission to lead, you might never do the work that matters most right now.

Develop Your Risk Assessment Framework

Instead of jumping straight into formal compliance matrices, start with a practical risk assessment framework – a consistent way to think through trade-offs systematically. You can always build more sophisticated tools later, but this approach can help you make better decisions immediately.

Key Questions:

- What's the worst realistic outcome if this goes wrong?
- How likely is that outcome?
- What would it cost to prevent versus fix?
- Is this a one-time decision or does this set a precedent?

Document Your Reasoning

Document your reasoning, even if your decision turns out wrong. Showing that you thought it through systematically builds credibility.

> **Example:** *"I approved this campaign because: (1) we have clear consent for this use, (2) the unsubscribe process is working, and (3) the audience matches our stated purposes. If we get complaints, we can point to these safeguards."*

Communicate Uncertainty Honestly

It's okay to communicate uncertainty honestly: *"This is my best assessment after consulting with our legal team and based on current information. Let's monitor for issues and adjust if needed."*

This kind of transparency builds trust and shows that you're making thoughtful decisions rather than just following scripts.

Your Starting Point – Building Your Foundation

As you begin building influence in your organization, focus on understanding the real networks and relationships that get privacy work done. This isn't about following a checklist; it's about developing the situational awareness and relationships that make privacy work sustainable.

Look for opportunities to make small privacy improvements that genuinely help other teams, not just advance your compliance agenda. These early wins build the credibility and goodwill that make larger privacy initiatives possible later.

Remember that visible progress often matters more than perfect compliance, especially early in your privacy work. Demonstrating practical value creates the foundation for everything else you'll need to accomplish.

Understanding the real network inside your organization – who actually gets things done and how – is the foundation of effective privacy work. The relationships you build now will determine what you're able to influence later.

CHAPTER 3:

MANAGING PRIVACY WORK IN PRACTICE

From Influence to Impact

Now comes the practical question: ***What privacy work actually matters, and how do you manage it effectively when everything feels urgent?***

Start by recognizing that not all privacy work matters equally. Some work has to be done regardless of business value. Other work directly affects business outcomes. And occasionally, privacy creates genuine strategic value. Knowing the difference changes how you prioritize, communicate, and measure success.

The Three Types of Privacy Work

Based on years of experience working with privacy professionals across different organizations, the work typically breaks down into three categories:

Type 1: Compliance Overhead (~50%)

What it includes:

- ☞ DSR processing and responses
- ☞ Vendor privacy assessments
- ☞ Policy updates for regulatory changes
- ☞ Cookie banner maintenance
- ☞ Mandatory role-specific privacy training

📌 **The reality:** This work is required regardless of business value. It's regulatory hygiene that keeps you out of legal trouble. There's no point trying to justify it as "strategic." It's compliance overhead, and that's fine.

📌 **The key:** Handle it efficiently so you have capacity for work that builds relationships and creates value.

Type 2: Business Decision Support (~40%)

What it includes:

- ☞ Reviewing new product features for privacy implications
- ☞ Advising on data use in marketing campaigns
- ☞ Evaluating privacy risks in business partnerships
- ☞ Supporting international expansion plans

📌 **The reality:** This is where privacy considerations actually affect business outcomes. Your input can improve decisions, reduce risk, or prevent problems. This is where you build credibility as a business partner and demonstrate value across functions.

📌 **The key:** Approach this work as an enabler, not a blocker. Your goal is not to stop projects, but to shape them so the business can move forward responsibly. Be concise, be clear, and translate risk into language business leaders understand. When you consistently show that you make projects safer and smarter, not slower, you build credibility that carries into every future conversation.

Type 3: Strategic Privacy Value Creation (~10%)

What it includes:

- Turning privacy compliance into competitive advantage
- Building customer trust through privacy leadership
- Enabling new business models through privacy-by-design

📌 **The reality:** These opportunities exist, but they're not as common as many people suggest. Most privacy work isn't strategic. When genuine value creation opportunities do arise, you'll have credibility to pursue them because you've handled the compliance overhead competently.

📌 **The key:** These opportunities are rare, so you must be ready to recognize them and act. They come when you've already earned trust through consistent execution. Treat them as high-leverage moments: a chance to align privacy with business strategy, brand reputation, or new revenue streams. If you oversell every routine task as "strategic," leaders will tune out. If you reserve that framing for genuine opportunities, they will listen.... and remember.

Risk, Perception, and Strategic Tradeoffs

This breakdown isn't fixed. It shifts depending on the company, its leadership, and the moment you're in. But one thing remains constant: not all privacy work matters equally at all times.

What gets prioritized often depends on how the company sees risk and how urgent something feels internally. A highly regulated company, especially one that faces audits regularly, may see updating its external privacy policy as the top priority. In contrast, a fast-moving business might accept a temporary delay on policy updates if it means getting quicker guidance on how to use data in a new product.

This is why even within that 50% of day-to-day work, not everything should be treated the same. Priorities have to adjust in response to both pressure and impact.

Perception often matters as much as priority. Just as important as what you do is how it's perceived.

If your team routinely delays answering real business questions because you're tied up editing policy language, people notice. It doesn't mean you say yes to every request. It means you think about how decisions are experienced by others. Saying, "We can't answer that until we finish updating the policy," might technically be true but unless there's an audit or regulator breathing down your neck, it can come across as disconnected from the business.

> Credibility isn't about being the most correct person in the room. It's about showing that you know what matters most in the moment, and why.

Privacy work often means navigating imperfect choices. You're constantly weighing short-term asks against long-term obligations. But if every answer defers to the slowest-moving priority, support starts to erode. So when you're making calls about where to focus, yes, consider risk but also consider relationships. The most effective privacy professionals stay anchored in the work that matters while staying connected to the people it impacts. Being responsive and thoughtful builds momentum.

Navigating Cross-Functional Dynamics

Different functions have different priorities, pressures, and success metrics, which means they'll need different types of support from you. Understanding how each function approaches privacy will help you tailor your approach and build more effective relationships.

Working with Marketing

What they care about: Lead generation, campaign performance, customer acquisition costs

Common friction points: Privacy requirements that limit targeting and consent steps that reduce conversions

Your approach: Help them understand which data uses are high-risk versus low-risk, and work together to find privacy-compliant alternatives that still meet their goals.

**Success Story:
A "Win-Back" Series That Improved
Engagement Rates**

When marketing wanted to re-engage lapsed customers, instead of saying "you can't email people who haven't engaged," we helped them create a "win-back" series that started with a preference center update request. Customers could choose to re-engage or opt out completely, improving both compliance and engagement rates. The key was framing it as an optimization opportunity rather than a compliance burden.

Working with Product

What they care about: User experience, development velocity, customer satisfaction

Your approach: Get involved in planning before features are designed. Show how privacy-by-design improves user experience and help them see privacy features as competitive advantages.

Success Story:
Simple User Interface that Reduced Support Tickets

During early planning for a new personalization engine, we proposed adding a simple user preference center rather than burying settings deep in the interface. Product liked that it reduced support tickets and gave users more confidence in the feature. Framing it as a UX enhancement, not a legal obligation, made it easier to prioritize.

Working with Sales

What they care about: Lead quality, sales cycle efficiency, competitive positioning

Your approach: Help them use privacy as a competitive advantage in sales conversations and train them to position privacy features as benefits.

Success Story:
A One-Page Privacy Document for Sales Use

The sales team was losing momentum when prospects asked detailed questions about data handling and security. We created a one-page privacy summary tailored for sales use: plain language, prospect-facing, and focused on how our practices reduce risk and support enterprise requirements. It became a standard part of their pitch deck and helped them handle objections with confidence, especially in regulated industries.

Creating Clear Ownership and Accountability

Privacy work stalls when no one knows who's responsible or when responsibility is too vague to act on. Ownership clarity protects both privacy outcomes and team bandwidth.

Be Specific Enough to Work

It's not enough to say, "Consent is managed by Marketing." That's a department, not a decision-maker.

You need actionable specificity:

> Vague: *"Marketing handles opt-outs."*
> Specific: *"Sarah Smith in Marketing Ops configures HubSpot opt-out preferences and tests them monthly."*

This makes accountability visible. It gives others someone to ask questions, coordinate with, or flag issues to. And it ensures nothing gets lost in translation.

But here's the balance: while naming individuals moves things forward today, your long-term documentation should tie accountability to roles, not just names. People change jobs. Roles persist. The trick is to hold both views:

> In your day-to-day work, name names.
> In your systems and artifacts, tie ownership to roles.

Connect to Existing Work

Privacy shouldn't feel like a new layer of work. It should show up in what people are already doing. Show how privacy fits into work people already do:

Function	Privacy Integration
Customer Service	When customers ask about their data, route to this queue and use this template
HR	When employees leave, follow this checklist for data cleanup
IT	Include these privacy questions in your existing vendor security review

Document and Communicate Decisions

When you make a call, write it down and tell people why. This builds precedent and reduces future confusion.

> **Example:** *"We agreed that user IP addresses will be retained for security logging but excluded from analytics reporting. I documented the decision in the data classification guide and flagged it in the next team sync to prevent future misalignment across tools."*

Celebrate Good Decisions

When someone proactively considers privacy, acknowledge it publicly. People generally repeat behaviors that get recognized, so acknowledging privacy-conscious choices publicly reinforces the behavior you want to see.

Managing Scope and Boundaries

Privacy professionals often become the default owner for anything related to data, risk, or compliance. While this shows trust, it can quickly overwhelm your capacity and dilute your effectiveness. Here are some suggestions on how to manage this reality.

When to Say Yes

- ✦ The request directly relates to personal data protection
- ✦ You have the expertise to add real value
- ✦ It builds relationships that help your core privacy work

When to Redirect

- ☞ The request requires expertise you don't have (cybersecurity, AI ethics, general compliance)
- ☞ It would prevent you from handling core privacy responsibilities
- ☞ There's a better-qualified person who should own it

Building Sustainable Systems

Look at how you're currently spending your time. If you're drowning in compliance overhead, that's normal, but see if you can streamline some processes to create space for relationship-building work.

If you're constantly putting out fires, consider which cross-functional relationship might help prevent some of those fires from starting. Sometimes strengthening one key partnership (for e.g., with marketing ops, product management, or IT) can dramatically reduce the number of urgent privacy questions that land on your desk.

Start Small, Build Systematically

When you do find opportunities to create clear ownership around privacy processes, take them. But don't try to document everything at once, as that generally is not sustainable. Pick the processes that cause the most confusion or create the most work for you and start there.

Remember: You're building something sustainable. Each relationship you strengthen, each process you clarify, and each small improvement you make creates momentum for the next one.

> **Key Takeaway.** Privacy work is ultimately about building systems that work for your teams under real constraints. While perfect compliance would be great, I've never seen that to be a reality. The goal becomes sustainable progress that reduces risk while enabling the business to move forward confidently. Success isn't about perfect compliance. It's about building systems your teams can sustain, under real-world pressure. If your organization can explain what it's doing, maintain it, and defend it, you're winning.

PART II:

DO THE WORK THAT MATTERS

In Part 1, you learned an approach to map the personal data in your organization. You've started to build credibility and capacity. Now comes the question: Where do you begin your work? What do you prioritize?

This isn't about creating the perfect privacy program. It's about building momentum with work that reduces risk, creates visible progress, and strengthens relationships. The goal is to sequence your efforts so they're not just defensible, but doable. In this Part we discuss how to prioritize strategically for maximum impact.

Why Starting with "Everything" Fails

Many privacy programs stall before they begin because they try to do everything at once.

Here's what typically happens: You step into the privacy role, feel overwhelmed by everything that needs attention, and default to the most comprehensive approach you can find. That usually means starting with a complete data inventory, detailed policy rewrites, and attempts to document every privacy risk.

In theory, that sounds thorough. In practice, it slows everything down. You end up cataloguing theoretical issues while real risks go unaddressed. Business needs evolve while you chase completeness, and people start avoiding you because every conversation turns into a project.

The result: Little progress toward sustainable, defensible privacy compliance.

Focus on What Creates Real Impact

A more effective approach starts with work that:

- Addresses real risk where sensitivity, scale, and visibility converge
- Aligns with readiness where stakeholders are engaged and systems can support change
- Builds credibility through visible progress that the organization can absorb
- Lays groundwork for scale by creating foundations that support future growth

Privacy risk isn't evenly distributed. It clusters in predictable areas:

- ☞ **Customer-facing operations** → What regulators and users see first
- ☞ **Revenue-driving activities** → Where it's hardest to pause and fix problems
- ☞ **Cross-border operations** → Where complexity compounds quickly
- ☞ **High-volume data flows** → Where small gaps become large exposures

But even when risks are clear, not every privacy initiative will gain traction. Some will move quickly. Others will stall in review cycles, tech limitations, or lack of stakeholder buy-in.

That's why it helps to look not just at what needs doing, but what's possible right now:

> **Are the stakeholders engaged or at least open?** Look for people who already care. It's easier to gain momentum with a willing partner than to convert someone who sees privacy as a blocker.
>
> **Is there someone who can approve and implement this change?** If decisions get stuck in committee or require executive sponsorship you don't yet have, it might not be your best first move.
>
> **Do we have the people or systems to make this work?** A solid idea with no resources won't get far. Start where current capacity supports execution.
>
> **Can the technology support it?** If the fix requires a major platform overhaul, it might be better in a future phase.

The same principle that guided building your internal systems applies here: **start small, move fast, and build credibility as you go.** This doesn't mean avoiding complex work. It means sequencing based on timing and traction. You're not just solving problems – you're building credibility. And credibility grows fastest when you deliver value in ways the organization can actually absorb.

The Work That Moves the Needle

The following chapters focus on four areas that consistently deliver traction and form the foundation for sustainable privacy programs:

Activity Mapping & Data Use → Understanding how data flows through the business, not just where it sits

User-Facing Experiences → Prioritizing what customers and regulators see first – your notice, cookie banner, and unsubscribe process

Privacy Request Handling → Building reliable, user-friendly systems to respond to data subject requests

Vendor Risk Management → Focusing on high-risk vendors with strong contracts and operational visibility

Each of these areas targets real risk, builds on organizational readiness, and creates visible progress that strengthens your position for more complex work later.

Rather than pursuing theoretical completeness, the following chapters focus on practical execution that creates momentum. The most important question in any privacy program isn't "What should we eventually do?" It's "What's happening with our data right now, and who's touching it?"

That's where we begin.

CHAPTER 4:

MAP ACTIVITIES, NOT DATA

A Practical Way to Understand Data Without Boiling the Ocean

If you've been told to start your privacy program with a comprehensive data inventory, you might want to reconsider that approach. A full inventory may sound like the gold standard, but in most organizations, it delays progress and obscures what matters most.

This advice typically comes from privacy textbooks, conference presentations, and Privacy 101 resources grounded in theory rather than practice. It sounds responsible, feels logical, and looks impressive in audit reports. But here's what I've observed happens in the real world: You create a spreadsheet with fifteen columns and send it to twelve stakeholders. Nine ignore it, three send back incomplete information, and it sits on a digital shelf, never updated. Nothing meaningful changes.

Maybe you've purchased privacy technology that promises to streamline your data mapping and privacy workflows. The sales demo looked impressive with automated data discovery, workflow management, and beautiful dashboards. But after months of implementation, you're realizing that the technology amplifies whatever foundation you already have. If your processes are unclear and your stakeholders aren't aligned, the software just automates the chaos.

Here's what we've learned over the years: A full data inventory is typically a result, not a starting point. Whether you're using spreadsheets or expensive software, if you don't already have credibility and organizational alignment, you'll likely spend months collecting theoretical data that no one uses to make actual decisions.

Instead, **map what people actually do with data.**

Most privacy programs start by asking: "What data do we collect?" This question often sends people into analysis paralysis. They start thinking about every database field, every log file, every cookie parameter, every form submission, and every API endpoint. The result? Overwhelming complexity that obscures rather than clarifies risk.

We've found it more productive to ask: **"What do we do with personal data here?"**

Starting with activities instead of systems works better because activities are:

- Observable (you can watch them happen)
- Repeatable (they follow patterns you can document)
- Business-aligned (they connect to actual work processes)
- Risk-revealing (they expose where things can go wrong)

Consider how these approaches play out differently.

When you focus on activities – like marketing campaigns, customer service processes, and HR onboarding – you quickly uncover:

- What data is used
- Why it's used

- Who's involved
- Where the biggest risks and opportunities lie

This activity-based approach surfaces meaningful insights faster, aligns with how the business already operates, and highlights where privacy can support rather than slow down critical work. It also gives you enough visibility to prioritize action without requiring perfect information.

A data-first approach produces lists like: "We collect names, emails, phone numbers, addresses, purchase history, browsing data, device IDs, IP addresses, cookie preferences..." This tells you what exists but not why it matters or how it's used.

An activity-first approach identifies specific processes:

- "We send welcome emails to new customers"
- "We run targeted ads based on website behavior"
- "We store employee performance reviews in shared folders"
- "We use third-party tools to track customer support interactions"
- "We use AI to score sales leads"
- "We automate content recommendations based on user behavior"

From these activities, you can ask smarter questions that reveal the data involved, the people accessing it, and the actual risks. You're building understanding that connects to business reality rather than creating abstract documentation.

Focus on Critical Flows First

Most privacy risk tends to be concentrated in a handful of high-impact activities. You don't need a full inventory to spot them. You just need to know where to look.

Common risk hotspots include:

- ➢ Marketing automation – Tracking, profiling, and opt-out mechanisms are often inconsistent or nontransparent.
- ➢ Customer support platforms – Agents may access sensitive data across systems with weak access controls.
- ➢ HR workflows – Personal data is handled heavily, but retention and access practices are rarely reviewed.
- ➢ Shared drives and cloud storage – Redundant and forgotten data lingers indefinitely, often unmonitored.
- ➢ Third-party integrations – Vendor risk often hides in operational shortcuts and unclear data flows.
- ➢ AI-powered systems – Automated decision-making, profiling, and opaque logic introduce overlapping risks.

AI-powered activities deserve special attention. They often bundle multiple risk factors: profiling, bias, lack of explainability, and decisions made without human review. These systems affect people directly and carry regulatory scrutiny.

Start With 3–5 Key Activities

Choose a few critical workflows or business functions to begin with. For each one, map the basics:

- ☞ What personal data flows in and out?
- ☞ Where is it stored or processed?
- ☞ Who has access?
- ☞ What decisions are made using that data?
- ☞ What could go wrong?

AI and Automated Decision-Making: Special Considerations

Why AI Activities Need Different Questions

AI-powered activities create unique privacy considerations that traditional data mapping often misses. Unlike manual processes where humans make decisions, AI systems can process vast amounts of personal data to make predictions, recommendations, or decisions with limited human oversight.

Key questions for AI-powered activities:

- ☞ What decisions does the AI make or influence? (hiring, pricing, content delivery, eligibility)
- ☞ What personal data trains the AI? (historical decisions, behavioral patterns, demographic information)
- ☞ How much human oversight exists? (fully automated, human review, human-in-the-loop)
- ☞ Can individuals understand or challenge AI decisions? (explainability, appeal processes)
- ☞ What happens to personal data in AI training? (retention, anonymization, model updates)

Common AI Activities to Map

- ☞ **Customer-facing AI:** Chatbots that collect personal information, recommendation engines that profile user behavior, personalization systems that track preferences, automated customer service routing based on account information.
- ☞ **Internal AI systems:** Resume screening tools used by HR, sales lead scoring based on demographic and behavioral data, employee performance monitoring using productivity metrics, automated expense approval using spending patterns.

- **Marketing AI:** Dynamic pricing based on user behavior, audience segmentation using personal characteristics, ad targeting using purchase history and browsing data, campaign optimization using engagement patterns.
- **Risk and fraud AI:** Credit scoring using financial and personal data, identity verification using biometric information, fraud detection using transaction patterns, compliance monitoring using communication analysis.

Activity Mapping in Practice

Let's walk through a working example: the customer onboarding process.

Instead of cataloging every data point, consider mapping the activity flow:

1. Lead Generation → Prospects fill out contact forms on website
2. Initial Outreach → Sales team receives leads, adds to CRM
3. Qualification → Sales reps enrich contact data, schedule demos
4. Conversion → Customers sign contracts, added to billing system
5. Onboarding → Welcome emails, account creation, training scheduling
6. Ongoing Relationship → Regular check-ins, feature usage tracking, renewals

Now you might ask for each step:

- What personal data is needed?
- Where does it go?
- Who accesses it?
- How long is it kept?
- What rights do individuals have?

For AI-enhanced processes, consider adding:

- What automated decisions happen at each step?
- How does AI influence human decisions?

- What personal data feeds into AI systems?
- Can customers opt out of AI processing?

This approach gives you a meaningful view of data flows that connects to business reality rather than an abstract inventory that sits unused.

Leverage What Already Exists

Most companies are already documenting useful information in process flowcharts, vendor lists and contracts, IT system inventories, training materials, risk assessments, and customer journey maps.

For AI activities, also look for: Algorithm documentation, AI vendor contracts and assessments, model training procedures, automated decision-making policies, and AI governance frameworks.

Rather than reinventing the wheel, consider combining and translating existing documentation through a privacy lens. Your role isn't necessarily to create more paperwork; your role is to make existing information actionable for privacy decisions.

Field insight: A privacy professional was struggling to map customer data flows at her software company. Instead of starting from scratch, she found that the customer success team had already created detailed onboarding flowcharts for training purposes.

She spent an hour with the team lead adding privacy context to their existing documentation, identifying where personal data was collected, stored, and accessed at each step. When they discussed their new lead scoring AI, she added questions about what data fed the algorithm and how scores influenced sales outreach. This gave her a complete customer data map in a fraction of the time it would have taken to build from nothing.

Make It Visible, Not Perfect

You're not writing a regulatory filing. You're building a working tool that you and your stakeholders will actually use.

In my consulting company, BlueSkyPrivacy, we've found it helpful to use simple formats like tables, bullet lists, and one-page summaries rather than complex documentation that nobody reads. As AI evolves into practical use cases in organizations, these formats will certainly evolve.

- Highlight assumptions by marking where you're making educated guesses.
- Flag missing information by being explicit about gaps rather than pretending you have complete knowledge.
- Share working drafts to get feedback early and often.
- Update incrementally by adding detail as you learn more.

At this stage, the goal isn't to "finish" your activity map. The goal is to start conversations that uncover risks and build shared understanding of how personal data actually moves through your organization.

Build Influence by Solving Problems

You can build organizational influence quickly by using your activity mapping work to solve something real.

- When DSR processes are broken, use your mapping to identify where customer data lives and who needs to act.
- When marketing is confused about consent, give them a one-page flowchart of what requires opt-in.
- When HR is holding decades of resumes, show them a simple retention schedule based on business need.

☞ When product teams are building AI features, help them understand what personal data the AI will use and what disclosures they need.

People don't remember your spreadsheets. They remember you as the person who made something easier, cleaner, or safer.

Sample Activity Documentation

Why This Manual Work Still Matters in an AI World

You might be wondering: "Why map activities manually when AI tools can discover and document data flows automatically?" It's a fair question, especially as privacy technology becomes more sophisticated.

Here's the reality: AI tools are powerful amplifiers, but they amplify whatever foundation you give them. An AI system can scan your infrastructure and produce impressive-looking data maps, but it can't tell you why that customer service process exists, whether the marketing team actually uses that data field, or if the sales team has found a workaround that bypasses your official systems.

The foundational work we're discussing here teaches you to think like a privacy professional. When you manually map a few key activities, you develop the judgment to know what questions to ask, what risks to prioritize, and what solutions will actually work in your organization. This experience becomes invaluable when you're configuring AI tools, interpreting their outputs, and making decisions based on their recommendations.

Think of it this way: you can use AI to generate a privacy policy in minutes, but without understanding what makes a good policy, you won't know if the output is legally sound or practically useful. The manual experience builds the expertise needed to prompt AI tools effectively, evaluate their outputs critically, and adapt their recommendations to your specific context.

These examples are intentionally simple and focused on building a foundation for privacy work, not creating comprehensive data governance documentation. You might start with basic mapping like shown below (you can always add more detail as your privacy program evolves – or as AI tools help you scale the process.)

Option 1: Detailed Single Activity Map

ACTIVITY: Customer Email Marketing

Business Purpose: Nurture leads and customers with relevant content

Data Used: Email addresses, names, company info, engagement history

Systems Involved: HubSpot (CRM), Mailchimp (email platform), Google Analytics

Team/Owner: Marketing Operations

Frequency: Weekly newsletters, monthly product updates, ad-hoc campaigns

Data Flow:

- Leads enter via website forms ⊠ HubSpot
- Weekly sync from HubSpot ⊠ Mailchimp
- Email campaigns sent via Mailchimp
- Engagement data flows back to HubSpot
- Unsubscribes processed in Mailchimp, synced to HubSpot

Key Privacy Considerations:

- Legal basis: Consent (for prospects), Legitimate interest (for customers)
- Retention: Active until unsubscribe + 2 years
- Rights: Unsubscribe link in all emails, deletion via support
- Risks: Opt-in not enforced, unclear consent records

Potential Improvements:

- Audit consent collection process
- Document unsubscribe workflow
- Review Mailchimp DPA

Option 2: AI-Enhanced Activity Map

ACTIVITY: Sales Lead Scoring

Business Purpose: Prioritize sales outreach based on conversion likelihood

Data Used: Contact information, company size, website behavior, past purchase history

Systems Involved: Salesforce (CRM), AI scoring tool (vendor), website analytics

Team/Owner: Sales Operations

AI Decision Type: Automated scoring with human review of high-priority leads

Data Flow:

- Lead data enters Salesforce from multiple sources
- AI tool processes lead characteristics and behavior data
- Algorithm generates numerical scores (1-100)
- Sales team receives prioritized lead lists
- Human reviews leads scored above 80

Key Privacy Considerations:

- Legal basis: Legitimate interest (for business contacts)
- AI transparency: Limited - sales team knows scores but not methodology
- Individual rights: No current process for AI decision appeals
- Retention: Lead data retained for 2 years post-last interaction
- Risks: Potential bias in scoring algorithm, unclear data sources

Potential Improvements:

- Review AI vendor contract for privacy terms
- Document AI decision-making process
- Establish procedure for lead scoring appeals
- Audit training data for potential bias

Option 3: Simple Table for Multiple Activities

Activity	Data Used	System/ Owner	AI Component	Key Risk	Potential Action
Email marketing	Email, name, engagement	Mailchimp/ Marketing	None	No confirmed opt-in	Fix signup flow
Customer support	Name, email, account details	Zendesk/ Support	Automated routing	All agents see everything	Review access controls
Lead scoring	Contact info, behavior	Salesforce/ Sales	AI scoring algorithm	No bias audit	Test for discrimination
Content recommendations	Browsing history, preferences	Website/ Product	ML recommendations	No user control	Add preference center
Employee reviews	Name, performance, salary	BambooHR/ HR	None	Files shared in Slack	Move to secure folder

Using These Formats Strategically

You might use the more detailed format when you need to understand one specific flow that's causing problems. Use the table when you want to get a quick overview of multiple activities and spot patterns.

Both approaches are intentionally basic. You're building a foundation, not a comprehensive data governance program. You can always add more sophistication – whether through additional manual documentation or by implementing AI-powered privacy tools that can scale this work.

The Foundation for Everything That Follows

This single activity map becomes your first privacy "asset" and can act as your foundation for everything that follows. It demonstrates that you understand how the business actually works and gives you credibility to tackle more complex privacy challenges.

Most importantly, it gives you the wisdom to effectively deploy sophisticated privacy technology or AI tools when you're ready. You'll know what questions to ask the technology, how to interpret its findings, and whether its recommendations make sense for your specific business context. The manual work teaches you to think strategically about privacy – a skill that becomes more valuable, not less, as automation takes over the routine tasks.

CHAPTER 5:

DON'T WRITE A POLICY YET. FIX THE USER EXPERIENCE FIRST

Why Your Cookie Banner and Privacy Notice Matter More Than Your Internal Policy

New privacy professionals often get handed a massive internal privacy policy template – sixty pages of definitions, principles, and cross-references – and are told: "Make sure this is updated."

In most cases, I suggest that you forget it. For now.

That policy is not where your credibility will come from. It is internal and no customer reads it. Most employees ignore it. And leadership doesn't generally care until there's a breach or an audit.

What actually signals demonstrable privacy compliance? The public-facing experiences that real people interact with: your privacy notices, your cookie banner, your unsubscribe process, and how you respond to basic questions like "What data do you have on me?"

These are the elements regulators and customers will evaluate first. In my experience, fixing them is your fastest path to making a meaningful impact.

Where Most Companies Are Actually Exposed

Privacy programs usually break down in predictable places that create real business and regulatory risk.

User-Facing Experiences That Don't Match Reality

Your customer-facing privacy communications don't accurately reflect what your organization actually does with personal data. Privacy notices get written once but business practices evolve continuously. Legal teams write notices based on what they think the business does, not what actually happens.

Field Insights:
A SaaS company's privacy notice said they "don't sell personal data," but their marketing team was using a lead enrichment service that technically qualified as a data sale under CCPA. Nobody connected the dots until a customer complained.

In another instance,an e-commerce site offered granular cookie choices through their banner, but the website loaded tracking pixels regardless of user selections. The settings didn't actually control anything.

Why this matters: Inaccurate privacy notices create direct regulatory exposure under laws requiring truthful disclosures. Misleading privacy communications undermine customer trust and make it impossible to respond accurately to data subject requests.

Section 1: Audit Your Current User Experience

Your Privacy Notice: Get the Basics Right

Most privacy notices are written to meet legal obligations, not to optimize user experience. But clarity and accuracy matter more than ever for both compliance and credibility.

Both U.S. state laws and the GDPR require plain language. The GDPR requires privacy notices to be concise, transparent, intelligible, and easily accessible. U.S. laws like the California Consumer Privacy Act (CCPA), Colorado Privacy Act, and Connecticut Data Privacy Act require clear, reasonably accessible notices written in plain, understandable language.

The regulatory environment is changing rapidly. While early attention focused on California, multiple U.S. states now enforce privacy notice requirements. Each state has variations in what must be disclosed, and regulators are beginning to audit notices for operational accuracy, not just formatting.

If You Work in Privacy Without a Legal Background

You're not expected to draft legal language. Your role is to make sure what's written reflects reality. Legal counsel will cover regulatory phrasing and jurisdictional nuances, but you're the one who ensures the privacy notice matches how your company actually operates. That's not secondary. It's essential.

Focus on these practical checks:

1. **Is it functional?** Test every link, inbox, and contact method listed. If it says to email privacy@company.com, make sure that inbox exists, is monitored, and has someone responsible for responding.

2 **Is it operationally accurate?** Avoid including blanket statements like "we do not sell personal information" if the organization uses platforms or technologies that could be interpreted as selling or sharing under applicable state laws. Review what's in place and flag anything that conflicts.

3 **Is the rights process real?** If the notice says people can submit a request and get a response in 45 days, test that process yourself. Follow it end to end. Can a regular person do it easily? Is the data actually accessible? Are timelines being met?

4 **Are location-specific sections accurate?** Notices often include language like "Your Virginia Rights" or "For Colorado Residents." Make sure those sections reflect your actual ability to fulfill them and that the listed rights match what your organization supports in practice.

A privacy notice isn't just a legal artifact. It's a public commitment. Your job is to make sure the organization can deliver on what it promises.

Section 2: Fix the Most Visible Compliance Gaps

Cookie Banners: Where Enforcement Is Focused

Compliance Quick Check. Test this scenario: Visit your website in private browsing, click "Reject All," then check if Google Analytics, Meta Pixel, or advertising networks still receive data. If yes, you're at enforcement risk.

The most critical element in cookie compliance is verifying what your banner actually does. While organizations often invest heavily in banner design and legal disclosures, many fail to test whether their websites behave according to legal requirements.

Enforcement has escalated dramatically, with regulators targeting both design and technical deficiencies. Recent enforcement actions across multiple jurisdictions have resulted in significant fines for violations, including providing easier paths to accept cookies than reject them, setting tracking cookies before users can opt out, failing to honor Global Privacy Control signals, and making cookie rejection unreasonably difficult.

Major technology companies and various other organizations have faced substantial penalties ranging from state-level fines to multi-million dollar and euro sanctions. These cases demonstrate that regulators are scrutinizing both the user experience design of consent banners and the underlying technical implementation, with particular focus on whether websites actually respect user choices and privacy signals in practice.

> **Recent Enforcement Actions Reflect a Significant Shift.** regulators are analyzing whether data collection tools behave lawfully in real time, not just whether the banner language looks compliant.

Learn from Regulatory Testing Methods

Rather than following specific technical steps that change over time, the most effective approach is to adopt the same testing methodology that regulators use when investigating cookie banner compliance.

Enforcement decisions from California, the EU, and other jurisdictions show that regulators typically visit websites in fresh browser sessions to check what cookies load before any user interaction, click "reject all" options to verify that tracking actually stops, enable privacy signals like GPC to confirm automatic detection and compliance, and use browser tools to monitor what data transfers occur regardless of stated banner controls.

The Honda, Todd Snyder, Healthline, and Sephora enforcement actions in California all describe specific testing methodologies that regulators used. These decisions provide a roadmap for the same testing you should conduct on your own properties.

What Regulators Are Actually Targeting

Based on 2024-2025 enforcement actions, regulators consistently fine organizations for:

Design patterns that manipulate choice:

- Bright "Accept All" buttons next to dim "Reject" text
- Multiple "Accept" options but only one "Reject" option
- Hiding rejection behind multiple clicks or small text

Technical non-compliance:

- Cookies set before consent is given
- Continuing to track after "Reject All" is clicked
- Essential vs. non-essential confusion (marketing cookies labeled as "necessary")
- Consent not passed to vendors (banner shows rejection but Google Analytics still receives data)

Missing opt-out mechanisms:

- No "Do Not Sell" links for applicable state visitors
- Difficult or broken consent withdrawal processes
- Failure to honor browser privacy signals like GPC

Global Privacy Control (GPC) Requirements

GPC is a browser signal that allows users to broadcast a global opt-out preference. When enabled, websites must automatically opt users out of data sales and sharing without requiring additional action.

States requiring GPC compliance include California, Colorado, Connecticut, Oregon, and Montana, with additional states adding requirements through 2025-2026. The enforcement reality is clear: In the recent California enforcement actions, companies were fined for failing to honor GPC signals, and multiple state attorneys general have sent enforcement letters to non-compliant companies.

When You Need IT Support

For comprehensive compliance, you'll likely need technical assistance with:

- **Tag management audits:** Reviewing what fires through Google Tag Manager, Adobe Launch, or similar platforms to ensure conditional loading based on consent.
- **Server-side tracking assessment:** Understanding what data collection happens before browsers even load and how it responds to consent choices.
- **Integration testing:** Verifying that consent choices are properly communicated to all analytics platforms, advertising networks, and marketing automation tools.
- **Cross-domain tracking evaluation:** Ensuring consent is properly shared between your domains and partner sites.

Who Can Help You

Consent management vendors should provide detailed implementation guidance, audit reports, and documentation showing how their platform handles consent signals, regional targeting, and cookie behavior. Strong vendors have a vested interest in client compliance, since gaps in implementation can affect their own reputation and legal exposure.

IT or development teams can answer technical implementation questions, such as:

- ☞ Which tracking scripts are set to load unconditionally versus conditionally based on consent?
- ☞ What happens server-side when a user rejects cookies or revokes consent?
- ☞ How does the organization handle consent for embedded content like YouTube, social feeds, or third-party widgets?

Web analytics providers (such as those offering measurement or audience insights tools) typically have compliance documentation and settings that support opt-out preferences. These platforms can often be configured to respect consent choices and pause data collection accordingly.

Website scanning and tag auditing tools can help detect unauthorized tracking, ungoverned pixels, or consent violations across live environments. These tools simulate user interactions, monitor how tags fire, and identify when tracking occurs without proper consent – providing a vital check on whether privacy settings are actually working as intended.

Each of these teams or tools supports a different layer of operational privacy. Working together, they help ensure that the organization's consent experience is not only legally compliant but technically sound and reliably enforced.

Testing Resources and Limitations

It's important to be aware that free scanning tools can help with basic cookie detection, but enforcement decisions show that regulators look beyond simple cookie counts. The basic cookie scanning tools generally only detect client-side cookies and miss server-side data collection, fingerprinting techniques, scripts that load conditionally after user interaction, and data sent via APIs or server-to-server connections.

Red Flags Requiring Immediate Action

Recent enforcement actions highlight these issues as top priorities for correction:

Scripts loading before consent is given → Implementations that trigger tracking before consent have been penalized.

Tracking continuing after "Reject All" is clicked → Consent banners must actually halt all data collection when decline is selected.

No clear distinction between essential and non-essential cookies → Misclassification of cookies has led to violations and fines.

Consent choices not passed to tracking platforms → Opt-out selections must be communicated to all third-party tools accurately.

Browser privacy signals not detected or honored → Ignoring user signals like Global Privacy Control has resulted in enforcement.

Excessive friction in the opt-out process → Requiring extra steps (e.g., ID verification or lengthy forms) has been deemed non-compliant.

Opt-out mechanism never tested or monitored → Regulators expect continuous testing and auditing of consent implementations.

Sharing sensitive health-related identifiers without consent → Passing health-related data (such as article titles or health conditions) without explicit opt-in has triggered significant enforcement.

These red flags underscore that a complete and enforceable consent model requires proper setup, rigorous testing, and ongoing monitoring, not just a visible banner.

Action needed: Make this a priority conversation with your technical team and vendors immediately.

The Unsubscribe Experience

This might be the most overlooked privacy risk in most organizations. Broken unsubscribe processes are a leading cause of enforcement actions.

Consider testing this yourself: Subscribe to your company's newsletter using a personal email address, then try to unsubscribe. I've found this exercise reveals issues that aren't apparent from internal reviews.

Common Unsubscribe Failures

The Black Hole: The link works, but emails keep coming because the unsubscribe only affects one list, not your entire database.

The Runaround: "Email us with 'UNSUBSCRIBE' in the subject line and allow 7-10 business days for processing."

The Upsell: "We've unsubscribed you from promotional emails. Would you like to update your preferences instead?" with no clear way to just leave.

The Broken Link: 404 error or "Sorry, something went wrong."

What Good Looks Like. A functional unsubscribe experience typically works immediately or within minutes, applies to all marketing communications from your company, doesn't require additional confirmation steps, includes a brief confirmation email, and honors the choice permanently.

Section 3: Build the Foundation for Ongoing Improvement

Be Ready for Basic Privacy Requests

You don't need a comprehensive DSR portal before you can handle basic requests professionally. But in my experience, you'll want to be prepared when someone emails: "What personal data do you have about me?"

The foundation is straightforward: have a working contact information in your privacy notice and know who can help you gather information from different systems when requests arrive.

This is where collaborative relationships from Chapter 2 pay off. The detailed process for handling data subject requests systematically comes in Chapter 7. For now, focus on being reachable and having a basic plan.

These Fixes Buy You Time and Trust

When your public-facing privacy experiences are clear, respectful, and functional, you accomplish several important things:

- **You build reliable working relationships** because marketing sees you solving problems rather than creating requirements, and IT sees you improving user experience rather than adding complexity.
- **You reduce immediate risk** by addressing the most visible compliance exposures – those that typically trigger enforcement attention.
- **You create audit credibility** because when regulators evaluate your privacy program, they often start with public-facing elements. Having these fundamentals right signals competence.

- **You buy time for deeper work** because with urgent, visible issues addressed, you can focus on building internal processes without constant crisis management.

CHAPTER 6:

BUILD A PRACTICAL DSR PROCESS

What's Good Enough to Start: Who to Involve, What to Document, What to Automate

Now that your user-facing experiences are solid, you're ready to build systematic DSR processes. If you've never processed a data subject request before, it can feel intimidating. Your mind starts racing with worst-case scenarios: What if they ask for everything we've ever collected? What if I miss something important? What if we can't actually delete the data?

Take a breath. The key to handling DSRs isn't perfection, it's consistency. You don't need enterprise-grade automation or a fancy portal to begin. You need a clear, reliable process you can actually run.

The DSR Automation Trap

Here's what happens when organizations rush to buy DSR automation tools without building the foundation first: they automate chaos.

While AI and automation tools are rapidly evolving and promise comprehensive DSR management, current market reality tells a different story. Auto-discovery can list the data locations you connect and authorize, but it does not produce the working DSR inventory you need. It misses sources without connectors or credentials, including niche SaaS and custom applications, and it is typically blind to backups, archives, and replicated logs.

It also does not assign accountable owners or link systems to the operational rules that drive requests, such as intake scope, subject-linking method, SLA timers, and evidence logging. Without those foundations, the platform accelerates partial pulls, duplicate tickets, and gaps in coverage, which leads to rework and deadline risk. Build the base first, then let automation execute it at speed.

Why AI Still Needs Human Intelligence in 2025

Current AI-powered DSR tools promise comprehensive automation, but industry experience reveals persistent gaps that no amount of artificial intelligence can bridge without foundational human knowledge:

Data Discovery Limitations: AI excels at finding structured data (customer records, email addresses) but struggles with:

- Unstructured data in custom applications
- Data stored in legacy systems without APIs
- Information embedded in documents, images, or non-standard formats
- Personal data in system logs, backup files, or archived communications

Context-Dependent Decisions: The integration of AI has correlated with a 40% increase in data privacy incidents, with 46% involving PII breaches. This isn't because AI is inherently flawed – it's because AI cannot make nuanced judgments about:

- ☞ Whether data qualifies as "personal" under specific regulatory contexts
- ☞ Legal holds that prevent deletion
- ☞ Business justifications for data retention
- ☞ Identity verification when requests come from unfamiliar sources
- ☞ Custom business logic that affects data handling

The Integration Reality: Even leading automation platforms require "technical developer support" and "complex data management" expertise. Many privacy teams find themselves "waiting in queue for in-house engineers that have other projects to juggle alongside privacy asks."

Consider Meta's recent experience: their attempt to automate 90% of risk assessments led to concerns from employees about "creating higher risks" when human oversight was reduced. Meanwhile, GDPR now requires "appropriate human review capabilities" for automated decision-making, limiting potential efficiency gains from full automation.

Lay Your Foundation First

Right now, you need three foundational elements that no AI can create for you:

1. **Defined ownership** of who does what when a request comes in.
2. **Working data flow maps** showing where personal data actually lives in your systems.
3. **Repeatable processes** with consistent steps that work even when you're the only person handling them.

While some software claims to automate data discovery, these tools still require the human knowledge and process foundation to work effectively. The most successful DSR automation implementations combine human-mapped data flows with AI-powered data retrieval and automated workflow coordination. but only after the foundation is built.

Build Foundation, Then Automate Intelligently

Build these foundations first. Even as AI tools become more powerful at data discovery and process automation, you'll need this operational foundation to make the most of those future capabilities. Better to automate a process that actually works than to make broken workflows faster.

This chapter builds directly on the activity mapping work from Chapter 4. Remember those data flow maps you created? Now they become your DSR roadmap.

> **Important Note.** Privacy law is a rapidly evolving area with new regulations, enforcement guidance, and court decisions emerging regularly. The approaches outlined here provide a practical starting framework focused on US privacy laws, though the operational principles apply internationally. If your organization operates in the EU or processes EU personal data, you should work with qualified legal counsel to ensure your specific DSR processes meet GDPR requirements and other applicable international privacy laws.

The DSR Reality Check

Before diving into process, let's set realistic expectations about what you're actually dealing with in 2025.

DSRs are more common and complex than most organizations expect. Privacy requests have been surging dramatically over the past few years. A typical company now handles a minimum of hundreds of requests annually. Each manually processed request requires 30-40 hours of work when handled without systematic processes or automation.

Request types follow predictable patterns but have different complexity profiles. Opt-out and deletion requests are the most common. While the action to delete data seems straightforward, complexity comes from legal retention requirements, technical system limitations, vendor coordination, and determining what can actually be deleted. Most deletion requests from customers are relatively simple account closures, but exceptions create significant operational challenges.

Access requests are growing, though they remain less common than deletion requests. These are operationally the most complex DSR type because they require judgment calls about data scope, format decisions, redaction requirements, and coordinating data from multiple systems into a coherent response that's useful to the individual.

Self-service should be your first priority, not your backup plan. Well-designed self-service can automatically handle a significant portion of privacy-related requests. When customers can manage their own data through account settings, privacy dashboards, or automated deletion flows, you avoid the manual DSR process entirely.

Multi-jurisdictional complexity is real. Companies operating across states or internationally face an increasingly complex web of requirements. At the time of writing, 19 US states now have comprehensive privacy laws, with multiple differences. Recent growth in data localization laws adds another layer of complexity that AI cannot navigate without human legal interpretation. When laws conflict, it's common to apply the most protective standard and document your decision-making process.

US companies with any international customers or operations should work with legal counsel to understand varying response timelines and procedural requirements across different jurisdictions, as these can differ significantly from US state law requirements.

The automation landscape is rapidly evolving, but foundations remain critical. Modern DSR automation platforms can dramatically reduce fulfillment costs and processing time through automated identity verification, data retrieval, and secure delivery. However, these tools still require the operational foundation of clear data mapping, defined ownership, and established processes to work effectively. Think of automation as amplifying your existing processes: good processes become great, but broken processes just break faster.

Documentation and process consistency matter as much as outcomes. Having a clear, systematic approach that you can demonstrate is crucial for compliance. Work with legal counsel to determine what constitutes reasonable efforts for your specific organization, especially as privacy enforcement continues to increase with more frequent lawsuits and regulatory actions.

Know your deadlines and plan accordingly. Under GDPR, you have 30 days to respond, extendable to 90 days for complex requests. Under CCPA and other US state laws, you have 45 days, extendable to 90 days. For CCPA, you must also confirm receipt within 10 business days. When operating across multiple jurisdictions, use the shortest applicable timeline.

Reality check: Build systematic manual processes, then automate. The goal isn't to manually handle every edge case perfectly from day one. The goal is to reduce manual requests through self-service, build systematic manual processes for remaining requests, and create the foundation for eventual automation as your volume and sophistication grow.

Set Up a Simple Request Intake

Start with the basics: a way for people to submit requests and for you to track them systematically.

Create a dedicated channel for receiving requests. You can use a dedicated email address like privacy@yourcompany.com with a shared inbox or folder system and auto-reply acknowledgment. Alternatively, add a simple web form to your privacy notice page that includes fields for name, email, type of request, and any relevant IDs, with form submissions going to your dedicated email.

Sample Data Request Form

```
Data Request Form

Name: [text field]

Email: [text field]

Request Type: [dropdown: Access my data, Delete my data,
Correct my data, Stop marketing emails, Other]

Location: [dropdown with US states, EU countries, and other
major regions]

Additional Details: [text area]

[Submit button]
```

Keep the form short. You're gathering enough information to process their request efficiently, not interrogating them. Collect their contact information, type of request, relevant identifiers like account email or order number, and location to help determine applicable law and response timeline.

Create a standard acknowledgment that you send immediately, or at least within 24-48 hours. Delays in acknowledgment are a common compliance trigger.

Sample Acknowledgment Template

```
Subject: We've received your data request

Hi [Name],

Thank you for contacting us about your personal data. We've received your request and will respond within [X] business days, as required by applicable privacy law.

Request details:

Type: [Access/Deletion/Correction/etc.]

Submitted: [Date]

Reference: [Internal tracking number]

If we need additional information to verify your identity or process your request, we'll contact you at this email address.

If you have questions about this request, please reply to this email.

Best regards,

[Your name]

Privacy Team

[Contact information]
```

Include key elements like a clear timeline (be realistic and don't promise what you can't deliver), a reference number for tracking and follow-up, contact method for questions, and identity verification notice that sets the expectation you may need to verify who they are.

Build Your DSR Systems and Data Location Map

This is where your activity mapping from Chapter 4 becomes invaluable. You don't need to find every possible trace of data to process DSRs. You just need to know where personal data typically lives in your organization and who can actually get that data for you.

Reality Check: Why "AI-Powered Data Discovery" Isn't Enough

Vendors market AI that can "automatically discover all personal data," but privacy professionals report persistent blind spots:

- **Custom Applications:** AI tools can't understand proprietary database schemas or business logic
- **Third-Party Systems:** Many SaaS platforms require manual API configuration
- **Backup and Archive Systems:** Often require separate discovery processes
- **Embedded Data:** Personal information in PDFs, images, or non-standard formats

Your data location map isn't just documentation – it's institutional knowledge that no AI currently possesses.

For now, don't worry about formal org charts or who "should" own each system according to the company directory. Focus on who actually has the login credentials, knows how to run the exports, and can get you the data within a reasonable timeframe.

The person listed as the "system administrator" might be someone who left six months ago. The "data owner" on paper might be a VP who's never logged into the platform. You need the marketing analyst who runs reports daily, the customer success manager who knows all the database quirks, or the IT person who actually maintains the system.

Ask direct questions: "When you need customer data from Salesforce, who do you go to?" "Who knows how to export ticket history from Zendesk?" "If I needed employee records pulled, who would actually do that work?"

Sample Data Location Map

Customer Data Systems

System	Owner	What's There	Access Method
CRM (HubSpot)	Sales Ops	Contact info, interaction history	Export contact record
Support platform (Zendesk)	Customer Success	Support tickets, communications	Search by email
Billing system (Stripe)	Finance	Payment details, invoices	Customer dashboard export
Email platform (Mailchimp)	Marketing	Email preferences, engagement	Subscriber export
AI recommendation engine	Product	User preferences, algorithmic scores	Vendor API required
Website analytics	Marketing	Behavioral data (IP-based)	No direct export available

Employee Data Systems

System	Owner	What's There	Access Method
HRIS (BambooHR)	HR	Employment records, performance	HR portal export
Payroll (Gusto)	Finance	Salary, tax info, benefits	Payroll system export
Resume screening AI	HR	Application scores, decision factors	Manual review with vendor
Email/Drive	IT	Work communications, files	IT assistance required
Slack	IT	Chat history, file shares	Slack export tools

Website User Data

System	Owner	What's There	Access Method
Google Analytics	Marketing	Behavioral data (anonymized)	No personal data export
Cookie/tracking tools	Marketing	Preferences, tracking data	Tool-specific export
Chatbot platform	Customer Success	Conversation logs, AI responses	Platform export tools
Contact forms	Marketing/Sales	Form submissions	Database query

AI System Note: For each AI tool, document what data it processes, whether individual-level access is possible, and whether training data can be modified or deleted. Some models can't remove data without full retraining.

Flag any systems that can't export or delete data easily, and document those limitations.

This approach gives you a working data location map that demonstrates systematic DSR handling while remaining manageable for your team. You can always expand and refine it as your program matures.

Build Workflows by Request Type

Different types of requests require different approaches. Build standard workflows for the most common scenarios.

Access Requests ("What data do you have about me?")

Reality check: Access requests are actually the most technically complex DSR type, though they're relatively rare. Access requests require judgment calls about what data to include, how to format it, what constitutes "personal data" versus business records, and how to make technical data understandable to individuals. Most organizations see far more deletion and opt-out requests than access requests.

Follow a consistent process: Verify identity when appropriate and required, search primary systems using your routing guide, check AI systems for algorithmic decisions or profiles, compile data into readable format, review for third-party data or confidential information, and send secure response with data export.

AI-Specific access considerations: Include any automated decisions made about the individual (hiring decisions, credit scoring, content recommendations). The "black box" problem directly conflicts with GDPR's transparency requirements – document what AI systems made decisions about individuals and whether decision logic can be explained. When possible, explain the factors that influenced AI decisions. Note that some AI systems may not store decision histories.

Choose appropriate response formats based on the data volume and sensitivity: PDF summaries work well for small amounts of data and are easy to password-protect. CSV or Excel exports are efficient for structured data and can be encrypted. Secure file sharing links are essential for large files, using platforms with expiration dates and download limits.

Never send personal data via unencrypted email: Use password protection, secure portals, or encrypted email. Work with IT and Security to establish approved methods for secure data transmission that meet your organization's security standards.

Deletion Requests ("Delete my data")

Reality check: Deletion requests are complex due to legal and technical exceptions, but they're also the most common type of DSR you'll encounter. Most deletion requests are straightforward ("delete my account"), but the complexity comes from navigating retention requirements, system limitations, and vendor coordination when exceptions apply.

Follow this standard process: Verify identity when appropriate, check with Legal regarding retention requirements, coordinate deletion across identified systems with system owners, note any AI system limitations, document actions taken and any limitations, and confirm completion to the data subject.

Common Deletion Complications

Legal retention requirements: Tax records, employment files, transaction records, and other data may be legally required to be retained for specific periods. Financial services, healthcare, and other regulated industries have extensive retention obligations.

Litigation holds and investigations: Any data subject to legal hold, regulatory investigation, or ongoing dispute cannot be deleted. This includes not just obvious litigation but also internal investigations, compliance reviews, or potential future claims.

Technical system limitations: Many platforms (especially older ones) don't actually delete data – they just mark it as "inactive" or "deleted" while keeping it in the database. Some backup systems can't selectively delete individual records. Cloud services may replicate data across multiple regions with different deletion capabilities.

Vendor and third-party challenges: Data shared with marketing platforms, payment processors, analytics tools, or other vendors requires coordination for deletion. Many vendors have their own deletion processes and timelines that don't align with your legal obligations.

AI-specific deletion challenges: AI systems trained on personal data present challenges for data deletion rights. Some AI systems cannot remove individual records from training datasets without retraining the entire model, which may be technically or economically infeasible. Machine learning models may "remember" patterns from deleted data even after removal. Federated learning systems may distribute data across multiple training environments.

Be transparent about these limitations: "We have deleted your data from our customer systems. Our recommendation AI cannot remove individual training data without retraining the entire model, but your future interactions will not be used for recommendations."

What "reasonable efforts" means for deletion: You're not required to delete data that's technically impossible to remove, legally required to be retained, or would require disproportionate effort. Document your decision-making process and be transparent with requesters about limitations.

Sample deletion response with limitations: "We have processed your deletion request and removed your personal data from our active customer systems, including our CRM, email marketing platform, and support ticket system. However, we are retaining the following data as required by law: [list specific categories and legal basis]. Additionally, our fraud prevention system cannot selectively remove individual training data without compromising security for all customers."

Work with Legal to understand key considerations, including legal holds for litigation, regulatory investigations, or compliance requirements that may prevent deletion; system limitations where some platforms don't allow complete deletion; backup policies and deletion capabilities; and coordination with vendors who may have copies of the data.

Identity Verification Approach

Under GDPR, use "reasonable measures" to verify identity without being "unduly burdensome." Under CCPA, verify "to a reasonable degree of certainty." Other US state laws use similar verification language. Work with Legal counsel to establish verification procedures appropriate for your organization, industry, and risk profile.

Consider verification when requests involve sensitive data categories, you have a genuine doubt about the requester's identity, requests come from unfamiliar email addresses, or requests seek access to financial, health, or other highly sensitive information.

Common verification methods include matching email addresses already in your systems, asking for account-specific information like order numbers or recent interaction dates, using existing account authentication by having them log in, or requesting additional contact information you have on file.

Generally avoid requesting government-issued ID for routine requests, asking for more sensitive information than the original request involves, or creating verification barriers that are more burdensome than the data being requested, unless Legal counsel advises otherwise.

Coordinate with your Legal team to establish verification standards, document your decision-making process, and create escalation procedures for complex or suspicious requests.

Track Everything Systematically

Build a comprehensive tracking system that captures operational detail and helps you improve your process over time:

DSR Tracking Table *(see table on the right side)*

The enhanced columns capture important operational information:

- **Location** helps track applicable law and timeline requirements
- **AI Systems** documents which automated systems were checked
- **Reference numbers** provide internal tracking using formats like DSR-001, DSR-002
- **Extension tracking** shows whether you used the allowed extension and why
- **Systems checked** documents the platforms you searched
- **Actions taken** records what you actually did
- **Completed by** shows who helped, building your internal network
- **Notes** capture process improvements for next time

Date Received	Request Type	Name	Email	Location	Reference #	Due Date	Extension Given	Status	Systems Checked	AI Systems	Actions Taken	Date Completed	Completed By	Notes
2025-06-15	Access	Jane Smith	jane@email.com	CA	DSR-001	2025-07-15	No	Complete	CRM, Support, Email	Recommendation AI	Exported contact record, support history	2025-07-10	Marketing Ops	Support tickets took longest to locate
2025-06-18	Deletion	John Doe	john@email.com	TX	DSR-002	2025-08-02	Yes (+15 days)	Complete	All customer systems	All AI systems	Deletion in progress	2025-07-30	Privacy Lead	AI training data cannot be removed

Know When to Escalate

Not every request fits the template. Escalate when:

- Employee data is involved
- Legal holds or litigation exist
- Requests span multiple jurisdictions
- Sensitive data categories are requested
- AI system limitations require vendor input
- Requests appear abusive or can't be fulfilled

Have clear paths: Who handles legal review? When do you involve IT? What vendor contacts do you need?

Review Monthly, Improve Continuously

Once a month, review your DSR log and ask yourself key questions to identify improvement opportunities:

- What's your average response time?
- Which systems are hardest to extract data from?
- Are AI systems creating consistent delays or challenges?
- Are deletion requests taking longer due to legal or technical complications?
- Are you seeing patterns in multi-state request complexity?
- What requests took longer than expected, and why?
- Are there patterns in the types of requests you're getting?
- What process improvements should you make?

This regular review helps you refine your process, identify training needs for system owners, and demonstrate continuous improvement to stakeholders who want to know that DSR handling is getting more efficient over time.

Field Insight: One of our clients learned the value of this review when she noticed that support ticket exports were consistently taking the longest time. After discussing with the customer success team, they discovered that their ticketing system required a specific search format that wasn't documented anywhere. Once they created a simple guide for searching by customer email, response times for access requests dropped by several days.

When DSR Automation Actually Helps

Don't throw automation under the bus entirely. Smart DSR automation can significantly improve your process – but only after you've built the foundation it needs to work effectively.

Smart DSR Automation Wins:

- **Workflow Management:** Automated routing, deadline tracking, and status updates
- **Identity Verification:** Matching against existing account data and standard verification steps, including features that automatically filter spam requests
- **Structured Data Retrieval:** Pulling customer records from well-integrated systems
- **Response Generation:** Creating standardized acknowledgments and status updates
- **Compliance Monitoring:** Tracking response times and generating audit logs

Foundation-Dependent Automation

The most successful DSR automation implementations combine:

- Human-mapped data flows (your foundation work)
- AI-powered data retrieval (from known, mapped systems)
- Automated workflow coordination (routing, tracking, communications)
- Human oversight for edge cases (complex legal determinations, unusual requests)

This hybrid approach can reduce manual workload by 70% while maintaining the quality oversight that pure automation cannot provide.

Build First, Automate Later

This is your minimum viable DSR process. You can automate later. You can buy enterprise tools later. As AI and automation capabilities evolve, they'll likely make data discovery and process coordination much more sophisticated, but they'll still need this operational foundation to work effectively. This foundation of clear intake, consistent acknowledgment, systematic response, and careful tracking will serve you well no matter how sophisticated your program becomes.

The goal isn't to handle every possible edge case perfectly from day one. It's to build a systematic approach that demonstrates good faith compliance efforts, creates consistency for requesters, and gives you the operational foundation to improve over time.

AI will make DSR processing faster and more efficient, but only if you first build the operational foundation that AI needs to work effectively. Skip the foundation, and you'll automate chaos at lightning speed.

Start with this basic framework, process a few requests to test your workflows, and refine based on what you learn. Pay attention to AI system challenges and multi-state complexity as you build experience. Expect deletion requests to be more complex than access requests. Most organizations find that once they have this foundation in place, DSR processing becomes much more manageable and predictable than they initially expected.

CHAPTER 7:

VENDORS: THE CRAWL-WALK-RUN APPROACH TO THIRD-PARTY RISK

The Current Enforcement Reality

Vendor oversight has become a primary enforcement target. Recent CCPA actions demonstrate that regulators are no longer treating third-party data processing as a secondary concern – they're scrutinizing whether organizations have proper service provider agreements, accurate disclosures about vendor relationships, and meaningful oversight of data processing activities.

The enforcement pattern is clear: inadequate vendor agreements and inaccurate disclosures about vendor relationships are generating regulatory penalties. This shift reflects a fundamental change in how privacy regulators view organizational accountability for third-party processing.

Strategic Approach: Focus First, Scale Later

Most privacy professionals delay vendor management because they assume it requires comprehensive vendor registries, detailed privacy impact assessments for every relationship, and becoming the gatekeeper for every new tool purchase. This "build everything first" approach typically results in months of planning with minimal risk reduction.

The more effective approach: start with strategic focus on existing relationships, then build scalable processes.

The Crawl-Walk-Run Framework

Crawl: Achieve visibility and assess basic privacy risk with current vendors. Focus on high-risk priorities first. You cannot manage risks you haven't identified.

Walk: Establish baseline protections and requirements. Work with legal to develop contracts, data processing agreements, and key assessments for your most important vendor relationships.

Run: Create scalable vendor risk workflows. Build processes for new vendor onboarding and ongoing monitoring that operate without constant manual intervention.

Immediate Actions: Establish lear Boundaries

1. Identify Your Critical Five

Select your five most critical vendor relationships involving personal data, prioritizing those that:

- Process large volumes of customer data
- Handle sensitive data categories
- Are customer-facing or deeply integrated with core systems
- Would be difficult to replace quickly
- Present the highest regulatory risk given current enforcement patterns

2. Verify Contractual Protections

For each critical vendor, ensure contracts clearly define:

Classification and Scope:

- Whether the vendor is a service provider or if data sharing constitutes a "sale" under applicable privacy laws
- Specific business purposes for data processing
- Restrictions on use, retention, or disclosure of your data

Operational Requirements:

- Required certifications that the vendor will not sell, share, or use personal information outside defined business purposes
- Data security and breach notification requirements
- Your right to audit vendor compliance and terminate for violations

3. Align Disclosures with Reality

Review your privacy notice disclosures to ensure they accurately reflect your vendor relationships, particularly any that might qualify as data sales or sharing under state privacy laws. Vague or overly broad purposes will not withstand regulatory scrutiny.

4. Document Business Justification

For each data sharing relationship, document the specific business purpose. This documentation should be precise enough to demonstrate legitimate business need and regulatory compliance.

Building Foundation for Scale

This tactical approach addresses immediate compliance risks while creating the foundation for more comprehensive vendor management. Once you have visibility into your critical vendor relationships and appropriate protections in place, you can systematically expand to broader vendor populations and more sophisticated risk management processes.

Important Note. Vendor privacy requirements vary significantly by jurisdiction, industry, and business model. Privacy laws continue to evolve regarding third-party data processing, international transfers, and vendor accountability, including rapidly developing requirements around AI processing, algorithmic decision-making, and automated systems. The approaches outlined here provide operational guidance for getting started, but work with qualified legal counsel to ensure your vendor management practices meet current legal requirements in your specific context.

Step 1: Discover Your Actual Vendor Landscape

Start With Finance (But Don't Stop There)

Many privacy professionals recommend beginning with Finance or Procurement because they maintain records of who's actually being paid. This is smart. If money is flowing to a vendor, there's likely a formal relationship worth reviewing.

Finance can tell you about vendors with formal contracts and regular payments, subscription services and SaaS platforms, major technology partnerships, and officially approved vendor relationships. But Finance only shows part of the picture.

The Hidden Vendor Problem

Many privacy-relevant vendors never touch the official procurement process. Free tools and freemium platforms, individual team subscriptions paid with corporate cards, trial software that became permanent without formal approval, AI tools and browser extensions that teams add individually, and third-party integrations within approved platforms all handle data but bypass traditional vendor management.

> **The complete discovery approach:** Get the Finance list first, then go directly to teams and ask people doing the work.

Talk to Teams Directly

Have a fifteen-minute conversation with each team lead rather than sending a spreadsheet.

Try this approach: *"I'm working on understanding what third-party tools we use that might handle customer or employee data. This includes AI tools, automation platforms, and any services that analyze or make decisions about data. Can you walk me through the main platforms your team uses day-to-day?"*

What Each Team Typically Uses

IT/Operations typically uses cloud platforms like AWS, Google Cloud, or Azure; productivity tools like Google Workspace or Microsoft 365; communication platforms like Slack, Teams, or Zoom; AI development platforms and machine learning services; and storage and backup services.

Marketing commonly uses analytics platforms like Google Analytics or Adobe Analytics; email marketing tools like Mailchimp, HubSpot, or Constant Contact; social media management tools; advertising platforms like Facebook Ads or LinkedIn Ads; AI-powered content generation, personalization engines, and predictive analytics tools; and lead generation and enrichment tools.

Sales relies on CRM systems like Salesforce, HubSpot, or Pipedrive; prospecting tools like ZoomInfo, Outreach, or SalesLoft; video calling and demo platforms; AI-powered sales scoring, conversation analysis, and lead qualification tools; and proposal and contract platforms.

HR uses HRIS platforms like BambooHR, Workday, or ADP; recruiting tools like Greenhouse, Lever, or Indeed; benefits administration systems; performance management tools; AI resume screening, interview analysis, and employee sentiment tools; and background check services.

Customer Success and Support depends on help desk platforms like Zendesk, Intercom, or Freshdesk; live chat tools; knowledge base platforms; AI chatbots, sentiment analysis, and automated response systems; and customer feedback tools.

Essential Follow-Up Questions

- Does that tool store customer information?
- Do you upload lists or export data from other systems?
- Does the tool use AI to analyze data or make automated decisions about people?
- Who set up the tool and do we have a contract with them?
- Are there any tools you're testing or considering?

You'll get much more complete information this way than from any formal vendor list.

Step 2:
Triage by Risk Level

You don't need to review every vendor with the same intensity. Focus your energy where the privacy risk is highest.

High-risk vendors require immediate attention and include those that process large volumes of personal data like CRMs, email platforms, and analytics tools; handle sensitive data like HR systems, payment processors, and background check services; use AI to make decisions about individuals or process personal data for training; provide customer-facing platforms like support tools, marketing automation, and website chat; involve cross-border data transfers; or have broad data access like productivity suites and cloud storage with wide employee access.

Medium-risk vendors can be reviewed second and include tools with limited personal data like project management platforms with some user information; platforms used for specific use cases like event management or survey tools used occasionally; AI tools that process anonymized or aggregated data without individual decision-making; and internal-only tools like expense management and time tracking.

Lower-risk vendors can be reviewed later and include those with no personal data like design tools and development platforms with no user data; tools that only process anonymized data like some analytics platforms; and infrastructure services with no data access like DNS services and CDNs.

Create a basic vendor risk assessment table to organize your findings:

Sample Vendor Risk Assessment

Vendor	Personal Data?	Sensitive Data?	Customer-Facing?	AI/Automated Decisions?	International?	Risk Level
Salesforce	Yes - High volume	Some financial	Yes	Lead scoring	Yes	HIGH
HireVue	Yes - Video interviews	Yes - Hiring decisions	No	Yes - AI screening	Yes	HIGH
Slack	Yes - Communications	Some confidential	No	Minimal	Yes	MEDIUM
Zoom	Yes - Names, emails	No	Sometimes	Minimal	Yes	MEDIUM
Figma	Minimal	No	No	No	Yes	LOW
GitHub	Minimal personal	No	No	Code analysis only	Yes	LOW

Step 3: Locate and Review Key Contracts

For your high-risk vendors, find the actual agreements. You're looking for the Master Service Agreement or main contract, Data Processing Addendum or Data Processing Agreement, AI Processing terms or Machine Learning addendums, their Privacy Policy, and security documentation like SOC 2 reports or security questionnaires.

Watch for red flags in contracts, including no DPA for vendors processing personal data, unlimited data use rights, unclear AI training or model development rights, no deletion commitments when the contract ends, weak security requirements or breach notification terms, no algorithmic transparency or bias mitigation commitments, and unlimited subprocessor rights.

Good vendor agreements include clear data processing scope that specifies what data is processed, for what purpose, and for how long; purpose limitations so the vendor can only use data for agreed services; individual rights support so the vendor will help with data subject requests; AI-specific protections including limits on training data use, algorithmic decision transparency, and bias monitoring; security requirements and audit rights; breach notification timelines; and clear data return or deletion processes.

Step 4: Conduct Focused Vendor Reviews

For many organizations, conducting in-depth reviews of every vendor is impractical. Instead of starting with lengthy, generic assessments, use a focused set of privacy-specific questions tailored to your actual data use. This approach is especially helpful for identifying red flags early and prioritizing follow-up with higher-risk vendors.

These questions are not a substitute for a full security or legal review, but they provide an operational baseline to ensure that core privacy risks – such as automated processing, international data transfers, and individual rights support – are identified and documented.

Sample Vendor Privacy Questionnaire

Data Handling

1. Do you access, store, or process personal data on our behalf?
2. What types of personal data do you handle for our account?
3. Where is our data stored and processed (countries or regions)?

AI and Automated Processing

4. Do you use AI, machine learning, or automated decision-making on our data?
5. If yes, what decisions are made automatically, and can individuals request human review?
6. Do you use our data to train AI models? If so, can we opt out?
7. How do you monitor for bias or discrimination in your automated systems?

International AI Considerations

U.S. companies are increasingly discovering that international AI regulations may apply even when operations appear domestic. The EU AI Act and similar frameworks introduce new obligations for transparency, fairness, and documentation. When evaluating AI vendors, ask whether they serve international markets and what compliance measures they have implemented. Work with legal counsel to understand which international requirements may apply to your specific AI use cases.

Security and Access

8. Who at your company can access our data, and how is access controlled?
9. Do you use subprocessors or third parties? If so, how do you assess and manage their risk?

Individual Rights

10. Can you support individual deletion and access requests? What is your process?
11. How do you handle our data when the contract ends?

Compliance

12. Can you provide a current SOC 2 report or other security certifications?
13. What is your process for notifying customers about security incidents?
14. Do you carry cyber insurance that covers data breaches?

Use shared tools like Google Forms or Typeform to streamline collection and improve response rates. Be clear about the purpose of your questionnaire: to identify privacy risk factors and prioritize deeper reviews where needed.

Request links to documentation instead of large attachments. Set a clear response deadline (typically two weeks) and follow up once before documenting non-responses as part of your vendor risk register.

This approach is a practical first step, not a comprehensive solution. Use it to surface risk indicators, streamline initial reviews, and focus resources where the risk is highest.

Step 5: Document Your Findings

Create a vendor risk register that captures what you've learned and helps you track ongoing management:

Sample Vendor Risk Register

Vendor	Data Types	AI Use	DPA Status	Key Risks	Last Reviewed	Next Action
Mailchimp	Email, names, engagement	**Predictive analytics**	Current	Marketing data retention unclear	2025-06-01	Review retention settings
ChatGPT Enterprise	Employee prompts, uploads	**Content generation**	Missing	Training data unclear	2025-06-10	Request AI processing terms
Zendesk	Support tickets, customer data	**Sentiment analysis**	Current	All agents have full access	2025-06-05	Discuss access controls
BambooHR	Employee records, performance	**Resume screening**	Missing	No DPA on file	2025-06-10	Request DPA from vendor
Google Analytics	Behavioral data, demographics	**Audience insights**	Built-in	Data sharing settings unclear	2025-06-01	Audit GA configuration

Color-code your risk register for quick visual reference. Red indicates high risk requiring immediate action, yellow shows medium risk to address within ninety days, and green represents low risk to monitor and review annually.

Step 6: Start With Quick Wins

Don't try to fix everything at once. Pick two or three specific improvements you can make this month.

Quick wins might include:

- Contacting vendors to execute missing Data Processing Addendums
- Requesting AI processing terms and training data opt-out
- Reviewing vendor settings to update unclear retention periods
- Working with IT to limit which employees can access vendor platforms
- Auditing AI tool configurations for data sharing settings
- Moving from email attachments to secure file sharing for sensitive data, or
- Requesting updated subprocessor lists from key vendors.

When vendor situations require additional support, know when to escalate:

- Contracts without DPAs may need Legal review for new terms.
- AI vendors making automated decisions about individuals may require additional legal review for algorithmic accountability requirements.
- High-risk vendors with poor security might need IT Security involvement.
- Vendors refusing to provide information could indicate the need to find alternatives
- International data transfer issues may require Legal guidance on transfer mechanisms.

Getting Unstuck: Practical Early Steps for Vendor Privacy Reviews

When organizations feel overwhelmed by vendor risk management, it's often because they're trying to go from zero to perfect. A more realistic approach is to build momentum by identifying a few high-impact actions that improve visibility and reduce obvious risk. These steps are based on what has worked in practice to help teams shift from stalled to making steady progress.

1 **Start with Discovery**. Talk to three or four teams that frequently work with vendors, such as marketing, IT, product, or procurement. Ask what platforms or tools they use that collect or process personal data. Pay special attention to any tools that use automation, AI, or machine learning. From these conversations, create a preliminary list of 15 to 20 vendors. Identify your top five based on factors like sensitivity of data, use of AI, volume of records, or regulatory exposure.

2 **Do a Basic Contract Check.** Locate contracts for your highest-priority vendors. Check for data processing agreements (DPAs), AI-related terms, and core privacy clauses. Even a quick review can help flag major issues, such as missing DPAs, vague processing terms, or inappropriate data reuse rights.

3 **Reach Out and Document**. Send focused privacy questionnaires to your top vendors, tailored to the type of processing they perform. For vendors using AI, ask specifically about model training, automated decisions, and opt-out options. Request any missing documentation and track responses in a simple risk register or spreadsheet.

4 **Tackle a Few Quick Wins**. Focus on two or three tangible improvements you can make right away. This might include getting a DPA in place for a key vendor, turning off unneeded data sharing features, or escalating a contract for legal review. Update your internal tracking so you know where things stand and what's still pending.

This approach helps you move from "we have no idea what vendors we're using" to "we understand where our top risks are and have started to address them." You are not building a fully mature vendor management program yet. You are building visibility, reducing obvious risks, and laying the foundation for a more robust program that can evolve over time. The goal is practical risk reduction through systematic discovery and focused improvements, not comprehensive vendor governance that takes months to implement and overwhelms your other privacy work.

CHAPTER 8:

AI GOVERNANCE FOR PRIVACY PROFESSIONALS

A Practical 30-Day Plan: From Zero to Working AI Governance

AI governance has fallen into your lap. You're probably feeling overwhelmed by technical complexity, regulatory uncertainty, and the pressure to "get it right" from day one.

Here's the reality: If you've been waiting for a global playbook on AI regulation, you've likely already lost ground. AI regulation isn't harmonizing – it's fragmenting. The EU AI Act, California's CPPA automated decision-making rules, and emerging state legislation are creating a patchwork of requirements that may never align.

This regulatory fragmentation makes leading with your company's values indispensable. When laws conflict or leave gaps, your values become the foundation for consistent decision-making across jurisdictions and use cases.

Most organizations try to build the perfect AI governance program upfront. That's how you spend six months in planning hell and ship nothing. Meanwhile, AI systems keep making decisions about real people with zero oversight.

> The goal isn't perfect AI governance from day one. It's building a working system anchored in your values that prevents disasters and creates credibility for everything that follows.

This chapter gives you a 30-day sprint to establish operational AI governance that actually works. You'll start with what matters most to your organization, identify your biggest risks, implement oversight for one critical system, and build the foundation for systematic AI management.

Before You Start: Lead with Values, Not Compliance

You don't have to build AI governance from scratch, but you do need to ground it in what matters to your organization.

Start with your company's values: What does your organization stand for regarding fairness, transparency, and individual rights? How do these values translate to automated decision-making about people? When regulations conflict or leave gaps, these values become your North Star.

Examples of values-driven AI principles:

- "We believe people deserve to understand decisions that affect them" → requires algorithmic transparency
- "We treat all customers fairly regardless of background" → demands bias monitoring and mitigation
- "We respect individual choice and autonomy" → creates rights to human review and opt-out

Extend your existing privacy processes: Your data protection impact assessments, vendor management frameworks, and data subject rights procedures already address many AI governance requirements. The challenge is adapting them to handle automated decision-making complexity.

Remember: AI amplifies existing privacy risks while adding new dimensions around algorithmic transparency and human oversight. You're not learning an entirely new discipline – you're applying privacy principles to a new technology context.

Week 1: Discover What You're Actually Governing

Find Every AI System in Your Organization

Start with an AI system inventory. You're not building a perfect catalog – you're finding what exists right now.

How to find them: Email department heads asking, "what automated tools do you use that make decisions about customers, employees, or business operations?" Review vendor contracts for AI-related services. Check with IT about SaaS tools with AI features. Ask customer service about automated routing or response systems.

Document these details for each system:

- System name and vendor
- Business function and department owner
- The decisions it make about individuals
- Data sources it uses
- Customer or employee-facing impact

Reality check: You'll discover AI tools people forgot they were using, systems people didn't realize were AI, and shadow IT implementations that bypass your normal approval processes.

Identify Your Highest-Risk Systems

Focus on Automated Decision-Making Technology (ADMT) – systems that make or significantly influence decisions about individuals.

Highest-priority ADMT systems:

- Hiring, promotions, or employment decisions
- Credit, lending, or financial eligibility
- Customer pricing or service terms
- Content moderation or account restrictions
- Insurance coverage or claims processing
- Marketing targeting that affects access to opportunities

Medium-priority systems:

- Customer service routing
- Product recommendations
- Fraud detection affecting service delivery
- Internal efficiency tools with individual impact

Week 1 Deliverable

A simple spreadsheet listing every AI system, its business owner, decision type, and risk level. Nothing fancy – just visibility into what you're actually governing.

Week 2: Choose Your Pilot System and Build Credibility

Pick ONE System to Govern First

Don't choose the most complex system. Choose the one that could create the biggest reputational disaster if it fails.

Ask yourself: What's the scariest headline I can imagine about our AI systems? That system becomes your pilot.

Examples of high-impact pilot systems:

- ☞ Resume screening that could discriminate in hiring
- ☞ Customer pricing algorithms that could create unfair treatment
- ☞ Content moderation that could amplify harmful content
- ☞ Fraud detection that wrongly blocks legitimate customers

Success here builds credibility for everything else. Teams will take AI governance seriously if you demonstrate value on a system they care about.

Conduct Focused Vendor Due Diligence

For your pilot system, apply these AI-specific vendor assessment questions:

Training Data and Model Development:

- ➢ Does the vendor use our data to train AI models?
- ➢ Can we opt out of training data use?
- ➢ What happens to our data if we terminate the contract?
- ➢ Are AI models shared across customers?

Algorithmic Transparency:

- Can the vendor explain how decisions are made about individuals?
- What factors influence automated decisions?
- How does the vendor monitor for bias or discrimination?
- Can we audit algorithmic outcomes?

Human Oversight and Control:

- What human review processes exist for automated decisions?
- Can individuals request human intervention?
- How quickly can we modify or stop automated processing?
- What controls do we have over system configuration?

Week 2 Deliverable

Complete vendor assessment for your pilot system and document gaps in current oversight or transparency.

Week 3: Build Your Minimum Viable Review Process

Create the Simplest Possible Approval Framework

Design a review process so simple that teams can't unnecessarily over-complicate it. Complexity can kill adoption.

Essential components:

- 1-2-page risk assessment form
- Clear yes/no criteria for launch approval
- Single decision-maker (not a committee)
- Maximum 1-hour review meeting

Core risk assessment questions:

- What decisions does this system make about individuals?
- What's the worst-case scenario if this system fails or discriminates?
- Can people meaningfully contest or appeal decisions?
- Is there adequate human oversight?
- Can individuals opt out of automated processing?

Decision criteria:

- **Green light:** Low individual impact, clear human oversight, transparent decision factors
- **Yellow light:** Moderate impact, requires additional safeguards or monitoring
- **Red light:** High individual impact without adequate transparency or appeal process

Establish Basic Transparency Requirements

For customer-facing systems: Update privacy notices to explain automated decision-making, decision types, and how people can opt out or request human review.

For internal systems: Document decision logic and oversight procedures for compliance and audit purposes.

Week 3 Deliverable

Documented review process and updated transparency documentation for your pilot system.

Week 4:
Test, Learn, and Iterate

Run Your First AI Review

Walk through the complete process with your pilot system team:

- Complete the risk assessment together
- Measure how long each step takes
- Document what feels bureaucratic or unclear
- Note where teams get stuck or confused

Fix problems immediately. If the process takes three hours, streamline it to 45 minutes by removing redundant questions and focusing on actual risks.

Build Your Appeal Process

Create a basic mechanism for people to contest automated decisions:

- Dedicated contact method (email address or web form)
- Clear routing to someone who can review AI outcomes with human judgment
- Commitment to response timeline
- Documentation of appeals and outcomes

Establish Ongoing Monitoring

For your pilot system:

- Monthly review of automated decision outcomes
- Quarterly bias and fairness assessment
- Annual vendor compliance review
- Incident response plan for algorithmic failures

Week 4 Deliverable

Successfully completed first AI system review with documented lessons learned and operational appeals process.

Building on Your 30-Day Foundation

Scale to Additional Systems

After proving your approach works:

- ☞ Apply the same review process to other high-risk systems
- ☞ Gradually expand to medium-priority systems
- ☞ Build team expertise through repetition

Enhance Vendor Management

For new AI vendors, ensure contracts include:

- ➢ Limits on training data use
- ➢ Requirements for decision transparency
- ➢ Audit rights for algorithmic outcomes
- ➢ Liability allocation for AI-related harms

For existing vendors: Review AI-related terms during renewal cycles and negotiate improvements where possible.

Adapt to Regulatory Evolution

AI governance requirements will continue to develop. Position yourself to adapt:

Stay informed about California's ADMT regulations, EU AI Act implementation, state-level AI legislation, and sector-specific AI requirements.

Build flexible processes that accommodate new requirements without complete redesign. Focus on transparency, human oversight, and vendor accountability as universal principles.

Document your approach to demonstrate systematic consideration of AI risks and proactive management.

When to Escalate Beyond Privacy

Legal escalation needed:

- ☞ AI systems affecting employment, credit, housing, or other legally protected areas
- ☞ Complaints about algorithmic bias or discrimination
- ☞ Inability to fulfill transparency requests about automated decisions
- ☞ Vendor contract disputes over AI rights or liability

Technical escalation needed:

- ➢ AI systems producing unexplainable or obviously biased outcomes
- ➢ Inability to extract individual data from AI systems for data subject requests
- ➢ AI vendors unable to provide adequate decision transparency

Business escalation needed:

- ✦ AI implementations creating significant liability exposure
- ✦ Customer complaints about automated decisions affecting service quality
- ✦ AI vendor relationships critical to operations but with inadequate privacy protections

Managing Ongoing AI Implementation Requests

When teams want new AI tools, use the "Yes, if.." framework discussed in the next chapter.

Marketing AI personalization: "Yes, if users can opt out and we disclose algorithmic targeting practices."

HR AI resume screening: "Yes, if candidates can request human review and we implement bias monitoring."

Customer service AI chatbots: "Yes, if customers can escalate to humans and we control training data use."

This approach maintains business momentum while ensuring appropriate governance.

What Success Looks Like After 30 Days

You should have:

- **One AI system under formal governance** with documented oversight
- **Clear review process** that takes under one hour to complete
- **Buy-in from at least one product team** who sees governance as helpful, not bureaucratic
- **Executive awareness** of what you're building and why it matters

You don't need a sophisticated AI governance framework to manage AI privacy risks responsibly. You need systematic application of privacy principles to AI systems, clear vendor accountability, and basic transparency about automated decision-making.

The approaches in this chapter provide a practical starting framework, but AI regulatory requirements are evolving rapidly. Work with qualified legal counsel to ensure your governance practices meet current requirements in your jurisdiction.

Remember: It's always acceptable to acknowledge when AI governance exceeds your expertise and request additional support. Building effective AI governance is a team effort, not a solo performance.

Regulatory Reality Check. At the time of writing, California's CPPA has finalized automated decision-making regulations, the EU AI Act is being implemented, and multiple states are introducing AI-specific legislation. AI regulation isn't harmonizing – it's fragmenting. The 30-day approach here creates a foundation that can adapt to emerging requirements rather than trying to predict every future regulatory development.

CHAPTER 9:

PRIVACY IMPACT ASSESSMENTS – WHEN THE LAW REQUIRES FORMAL ASSESSMENTS

Build Systematic Risk Evaluation Without Drowning in Bureaucracy

If you've ever seen a privacy program collapse under the weight of hundreds of unfinished PIAs stuck in legal review, you'll understand why this chapter takes a different approach.

Most privacy professionals get told to "implement a PIA process" without understanding the trap they're walking into. Do a formal assessment for every new processing activity, every vendor, every product feature, and within months you'll have a backlog that frustrates the business and overwhelms your team.

The reality is more nuanced. Some situations require formal legal compliance assessments. Most don't. The key is knowing the difference and building processes that scale without creating bureaucratic nightmares.

Understanding the Terms: PIA vs DPIA

Privacy Impact Assessment (PIA): The broad term for systematic evaluation of privacy risks. Used globally and required by US federal law since 2002.

Data Protection Impact Assessment (DPIA): Originally from GDPR Article 35, but now adopted by multiple US state laws and other jurisdictions. Colorado, Virginia, and several other states specifically use "DPIA" terminology. The term is gaining favor in US corporate practice as organizations deal with multiple state requirements.

Fundamental Rights Impact Assessment (FRIA): New requirement under the EU AI Act for high-risk AI systems, effective August 2, 2026. Can be combined with DPIAs.

The core methodology is identical. You're systematically identifying privacy risks and mitigation measures. The differences lie in legal triggers, content requirements, and publication obligations.

The Privacy Tech Automation Reality Check

Before diving into process, let's address the current landscape: privacy technology platforms that have been around for years are rapidly embedding AI capabilities and making increasingly bold promises about automated risk assessment.

Established privacy platforms now market AI that can "automate your records of processing (RoPA) reports, privacy impact assessments, and data protection impact assessment aligning with global privacy regulations." These platforms also promise to "streamline the PIA process, ensuring regulatory compliance, and better protecting personal information." Some vendors claim their AI can handle legal interpretation and complex risk judgments.

Here's what these platforms actually do well and where the limitations persist:

What Privacy Tech Platforms Do Well

- ☞ **Template Management:** Creating and managing PIAs with "out-of-the-box templates based on GDPR, CCPA, LGPD, and other global regulations"
- ☞ **Workflow Automation:** Routing, deadline tracking, and status updates
- ☞ **Documentation Generation:** Automating "the generation of comprehensive DPIA reports, including the scope of the assessment, data processing activities analyzed, identified risks, and recommended mitigations
- ☞ **Basic Risk Flagging:** Automatically suggesting "risk flags, missing fields, and suggested actions"
- ☞ **Integration Capabilities:** Connecting with existing business systems to pull data and trigger assessments

Where Platform AI Claims Don't Match Reality (at least not yet)

Claim: AI can make complex legal and risk judgments.

Reality Check: Legal interpretation requires understanding of specific business context, industry regulations, and organizational risk tolerance that AI cannot replicate. When California's CPRA or Colorado's CPA requires assessment of "profiling" activities, AI cannot determine whether your specific marketing automation constitutes covered profiling under your business model.

Claim: "Automated PIAs eliminate the need for stakeholder involvement

Reality Check: PIAs require input from legal, business, and technical stakeholders who understand operational constraints. AI cannot replace the collaborative process of identifying mitigation strategies that actually work in your environment.

Claim: "Our platform can automatically determine risk levels for any processing activity"

Reality Check: Risk assessment depends on factors AI cannot evaluate: your organization's existing security controls, your customer base's expectations, your industry's regulatory enforcement patterns, and your business's ability to implement different mitigation measures.

The Automation Trap in Privacy Tech

The automation trap isn't unique to new AI tools. It's been a problem with privacy technology for years. The difference now is that AI capabilities are making the promises more ambitious and the potential for misplaced confidence higher.

What happens when you automate without foundations:

- Platforms generate comprehensive-looking assessments that miss actual risks specific to your business context
- Templates create false confidence in compliance while real operational gaps persist
- Stakeholders assume the technology "handled it" and don't engage meaningfully in risk assessment
- You end up with documentation that looks thorough but doesn't reflect operational reality
- Assessment backlogs pile up because the automated process creates more work than it eliminates

The persistent challenge: Whether it's a five-year-old privacy platform or the latest AI-enhanced tool, technology can only amplify the process foundation you give it. If your stakeholders don't understand what constitutes privacy risk in your specific context, automation will systematically miss the risks that matter most.

The smarter approach: Build your understanding of PIA methodology, risk assessment, and your organization's data practices first. Then use AI tools to scale and systematize the process you've already proven works.

The Threshold Assessment: Your First Line of Defense

Privacy programs you can actually explain and defend don't usually start with full PIAs. They start with lightweight threshold assessments that quickly identify which initiatives actually need formal review.

A threshold assessment is a simple screening tool, usually 10-20 questions, that helps you determine whether a full PIA is legally required or operationally warranted. New Zealand's Privacy Commissioner describes this as helping teams "quickly and easily identify projects with no, or minimal, information privacy implications."[1]

Sample Threshold Assessment Questions for US State Privacy Law Compliance

These sample questions should be adapted to your organization's language, systems, and risk profile. Focus on creating a process you can confidently stand behind rather than checking every theoretical compliance box.

---

1. https://www.privacy.org.nz/responsibilities/poupou-matatapu-doing-privacy-well/assessing-risk/

1. Will this initiative collect new categories of personal information?
2. Does this involve selling or sharing personal information with third parties?
3. Does this involve profiling that could produce legal or similarly significant effects on individuals?
4. Will this enable targeted advertising or behavioral profiling?
5. Does this process sensitive personal information (health, biometric, geolocation, financial)?
6. Does this make automated decisions that significantly affect consumers?
7. Will this process personal information of minors under 16?
8. Does this involve new AI or machine learning technologies?
9. Will this transfer personal information to new countries or jurisdictions?
10. Does this create large-scale processing of consumer data?
11. Will this significantly alter existing privacy practices or disclosures?
12. Does this involve new third-party processors or service providers?
13. Could unauthorized access to this data cause substantial harm to individuals?
14. Does this collect or process biometric identifiers or biometric information?
15. Will this track precise geolocation or movement patterns?
16. Would consumers find this data use surprising or difficult to understand?

The goal is quick screening to separate obvious "no PIA needed" projects from those requiring deeper evaluation. If you answer "yes" to multiple questions, consider a full PIA. If you get mostly "no" answers, document the threshold assessment and move forward.

This approach prevents the "PIA everything" trap that kills business momentum and creates unmanageable backlogs. You're not trying to identify every possible privacy nuance. You're creating a documented trail that demonstrates thoughtful evaluation of privacy implications before moving forward.

When stakeholders ask, "How did you decide this project didn't need a full assessment?" you want to show them a systematic evaluation that any reasonable person would consider thorough and appropriate.

When Full PIAs Are Actually Required

Understanding the legal landscape helps you focus formal assessments where they're actually mandated. This area is evolving rapidly and it's important to stay updated on legal developments.

GDPR/EU Requirements (Mandatory)

Under GDPR Article 35, DPIAs are required for high-risk processing, including:

- Large-scale systematic monitoring (like employee tracking systems)
- Large-scale processing of sensitive data (health, financial, biometric)
- Automated decision-making with legal effects (AI hiring tools, credit scoring)
- New technologies likely to result in high risk

EU AI Act (Current Implementation)

As of February 2, 2025, AI literacy obligations and certain AI prohibitions are now in effect.

By August 2, 2026, high-risk AI systems will require Fundamental Rights Impact Assessments (FRIAs) that can be combined with DPIAs:

- AI used in employment, recruitment, or worker management
- AI for critical infrastructure, healthcare, law enforcement
- Biometric identification and emotion recognition systems

US State Privacy Laws (19+ States)

California CPRA, Colorado CPA, Virginia VCDPA, and 16+ other states require assessments for targeted advertising and profiling activities, sale or sharing of personal data, processing sensitive personal information at scale, and automated decision-making affecting consumers.

NOTE: Recent state law amendments emphasize documenting your decision-making process– bias testing records, consent evidence, and impact assessments aren't just nice-to-haves, they're becoming explicit legal requirements.

Build a Practical PIA Process

The most sustainable approach combines lightweight screening with focused formal assessments for genuine legal requirements.

Embed Threshold Assessments in Existing Workflows

Rather than creating a parallel PIA approval process, build privacy screening into decisions teams are already making.

- **Product development:** Add threshold questions to existing feature review processes
- **Vendor onboarding:** Include privacy screening in procurement workflows
- **Marketing campaigns:** Build privacy checks into campaign approval processes
- **AI implementations:** Require threshold assessment before pilot launches

Use Regulator Templates for Required Assessments

When threshold assessments indicate formal PIAs are needed, start with proven frameworks rather than building from scratch.

CNIL (France) provides open-source PIA software that has been downloaded 70,000+ times and translated into 14 languages. It's specifically designed to avoid overwhelming users while meeting GDPR requirements[2].

Australia's OAIC offers practical PIA guidance with flexible templates designed for different risk levels and organizational sizes[3].

New Zealand's Privacy Commissioner provides simple, practical templates that focus on answering specific questions rather than creating comprehensive documentation[4].

Scale Based on Actual Risk

Not every PIA needs to be a 50-page report. Match assessment depth to risk level and legal requirements.

High-risk assessments (AI decision-making, large-scale sensitive data, new technologies) warrant comprehensive formal PIAs with stakeholder consultation, detailed risk analysis, and ongoing monitoring.

Medium-risk assessments (routine vendor implementations, standard marketing activities) can use simplified templates focused on identifying and mitigating obvious risks.

---

2. https://oecd-opsi.org/innovations/pia-tool/
3. https://www.oaic.gov.au/privacy/privacy-guidance-for-organisations-and-government-agencies/privacy-impact-assessments/guide-to-undertaking-privacy-impact-assessments
4. https://www.privacy.org.nz/publications/guidance-resources/privacy-impact-assessment-toolkit/

Low-risk assessments (minor system updates, internal process changes) may only need documented threshold assessments confirming minimal privacy implications.

AI-Specific Considerations

The AI landscape is changing rapidly and requires special attention to new requirements:

FRIA Integration

For organizations subject to both GDPR and AI Act requirements, conducting FRIAs in conjunction with DPIAs provides efficiency while meeting both regulatory frameworks.

US AI Developments

While the current administration in the US has mandated that the FTC pull back on its active enforcement around AI bias and algorithmic decision-making, many companies lead with their values and want to document their approach. And the States continue to lead in this area. For example, Connecticut's expansion of 'automated decisions' to include those made 'on behalf of' controllers means vendor algorithms and third-party AI tools may trigger assessment requirements even when you're not directly making the decisions.

Practical AI Questions for Threshold Assessments

- ☞ Will the AI system process personal data of customers, employees, or third parties?
- ☞ Are there risks related to discrimination, bias, or unfair treatment?
- ☞ Does the system make decisions with legal or significant effects on individuals?

- Can you explain how the AI system reaches its decisions?
- Do you have control over the AI system's training data and decision logic?

When to Use AI Tools in Your PIA Process

AI can help with PIA processes but only after you understand what you're automating:

Smart AI Applications

- **After you've run manual PIAs:** Use AI to standardize documentation and track deadlines
- **When you have volume:** AI workflow management becomes valuable when you're processing multiple assessments
- **For consistent formatting:** AI can help ensure all assessments follow the same structure and include required elements
- **For tracking and reporting:** AI dashboards can monitor PIA completion rates and flag overdue assessments

Avoid AI For:

- **Initial risk identification:** You need human judgment to identify genuine privacy risks in your specific context
- **Legal interpretation:** AI cannot determine the privacy laws for your specific situation
- **Stakeholder consultation:** The collaborative process of PIA development requires human engagement
- **Custom mitigation strategies:** Solutions must be tailored to your technical and business constraints

Avoid the Common Traps

The "Assess Everything" Trap

Requiring formal PIAs for every privacy-related decision creates backlogs that frustrate business teams and overwhelm privacy resources. Use threshold assessments to focus formal reviews on genuine legal requirements and significant risks.

The "Perfect Documentation" Trap

Comprehensive PIA reports that sit on digital shelves provide less value than concise assessments that inform actual decisions. Focus on documentation that helps teams make better privacy choices.

The "Technology Will Handle It" Trap

Automated systems require ongoing monitoring and adjustment to function correctly and organizations must have processes to validate AI outputs and ensure that assessments remain accurate. Privacy platforms can accelerate PIA processes, but they cannot replace the human judgment needed for meaningful risk assessment.

This is true whether you're using a five-year-old privacy platform with new AI features or a brand-new AI-first solution. The fundamental challenge remains: technology works from templates and algorithms, but meaningful privacy assessment requires understanding your specific business context, legal environment, and operational constraints.

The "Legal Review Bottleneck" Trap

If every PIA requires legal review, you'll create delays that make business teams avoid the process entirely. Reserve legal involvement for complex assessments with genuine legal implications.

Connect PIAs to Your Existing Work

If you've been following this book, you're already collecting much of the information PIAs require:

- ☞ Chapter 4's activity mapping provides the data flow analysis that forms the foundation of most PIAs
- ☞ Chapter 7's vendor assessments include most of the third-party risk evaluation needed for vendor-related PIAs
- ☞ Chapter 8's AI governance covers the automated decision-making analysis required for AI-related PIAs

Rather than creating separate PIA processes, build on the privacy infrastructure you're already developing. Start with threshold assessments for new initiatives rather than jumping straight to full PIAs. Use regulator templates for situations requiring formal assessment instead of building comprehensive frameworks from scratch.

Most importantly, build privacy assessment into existing business workflows rather than creating parallel approval processes that teams will avoid. Privacy impact assessment is a tool for making better decisions about privacy risk, not a compliance exercise that demonstrates how thorough your documentation can be.

When AI tools can genuinely help – after you've built the foundation – they can make your PIA process more efficient and consistent. But skip the foundation, and you'll automate confusion at lightning speed.

CHAPTER 10:

HANDLING BUSINESS REQUESTS WITHOUT LOSING YOUR MIND

The "Yes, if..." Method for Working With Stakeholders

One minute you're reviewing vendor contracts. The next, you've got a Slack message from Marketing asking if they can upload customer email lists to LinkedIn for lookalike audiences. Or Sales wants to demo a new lead enrichment tool. Or Product is adding a feature that lets users upload contact lists.

None of this was on your calendar. But this is where privacy actually happens, in the quick questions, urgent requests, and "can we just..." moments that show up in your inbox daily.

These aren't interruptions to your privacy work. They ARE your privacy work.

Say "no" too quickly? You lose credibility and people stop asking. Say "yes" without thinking? You expose the company to unnecessary risk. Say nothing? They'll proceed anyway and loop you in after problems emerge.

You need an approach that keeps conversations collaborative while ensuring risks are properly managed and decisions are made by people with appropriate authority.

Important Note. Privacy roles and authority vary significantly by jurisdiction and organization. In the EU, Data Protection Officers have specific legal protections and independence requirements under GDPR. In other jurisdictions, privacy professionals typically operate as advisors to business decision-makers. The approaches outlined here focus on effective privacy consultation while recognizing that ultimate business decisions rest with appropriate organizational leadership.

Why "Yes, If..." Enables Better Decisions

Most privacy professionals inadvertently default to responses that shut down collaboration.

The Lawyer Response: "Well, that depends on the legal basis for processing, whether we have proper consent mechanisms in place, and if this falls under legitimate interests..." This sounds like legal jargon nobody understands.

The Wall Response: "No, we can't do that. It's too risky." This positions you as the "Department of No" and people stop asking for guidance.

The "Yes, if..." approach works because it keeps conversations open, surfaces actual risks without lecturing about theoretical compliance, uses business language rather than legal terminology, and positions you as enabling informed decision-making rather than blocking initiatives.

Your role isn't to make final business decisions about risk tolerance. It's to ensure those decisions are made with full understanding of privacy implications.

The Framework in Action

Instead of making compliance decisions yourself, focus on providing the information business leaders need to make informed choices about privacy risk.

The structure: "We can support this initiative. To manage privacy requirements, we'd need to ________[specific conditions]. Here are the options and their implications..."

Marketing wants to run lookalike campaigns: "We can support the lookalike campaign. For compliance with privacy laws, we'd need clear opt-out language and should limit it to customers who haven't unsubscribed. Without these safeguards, we'd have regulatory exposure under GDPR and CCPA. What works best for your timeline and objectives?"

Sales wants to try lead enrichment: "We can evaluate this lead enrichment tool. I'll need to review their data sourcing practices and opt-out capabilities to assess compliance requirements. If they don't meet privacy standards, we'd need to consider alternative approaches or accept potential regulatory risk. Should I start the vendor review?"

Notice how this approach acknowledges their business objective, explains specific privacy requirements, outlines the consequences of different choices, and asks how they want to proceed. You're enabling informed decision-making rather than making the decision for them.

Handling Common Scenarios

Marketing: "Can we retarget website visitors with Facebook ads?"

"We can support retargeting campaigns. For compliance, we'd need to update our cookie banner to get proper consent for advertising cookies and limit retargeting to users who opted in. The alternative is accepting regulatory risk under privacy laws. Want me to check what changes we need in our banner setup and estimate the timeline?"

Marketing: "We want to send a 'win-back' email to everyone who hasn't engaged in 6 months."

"We can support re-engagement campaigns. For compliance, we'd include clear re-engagement language and easy permanent unsubscribe options, plus exclude anyone who previously unsubscribed from other campaigns. Without these protections, we risk spam complaints and regulatory issues. Should we draft compliant language together?"

Sales: "We want to import leads from a trade show and add them to our newsletter."

"We can support this lead import. If they specifically consented to email marketing beyond event follow-up, we can add them directly. If not, we'd need a 'permission to stay in touch' email first. The alternative is potential spam complaints and regulatory exposure. What consent did we collect at the trade show?"

Product: "We're adding user analytics to track feature usage and improve the product."

"We can support user analytics implementation. For compliance, we'd update our privacy notice to explain the analytics and give users control over tracking preferences, plus ensure we're only collecting data needed for product improvement. What level of user control fits your product vision?"

IT: "Can we integrate with Zapier to sync user data between platforms?"

"We can support Zapier integration. I'll need to review their data processing terms and ensure we limit the sync to necessary data for the specific workflow.

We'd also need to consider whether additional vendor disclosures are required. Should I start the privacy review while you plan the technical implementation?"

Each response follows the same pattern: acknowledge the business goal, explain specific privacy requirements, describe the implications of different approaches, and ask how they want to proceed.

Training Teams to Ask Early

The best privacy conversations happen during planning, not after implementation. Train teams to bring privacy questions early by providing a simple framework for identifying when privacy input is needed.

Help them recognize privacy considerations by asking: What personal data will this collect or use? Where will the data be stored? Does this involve a new vendor or third party? Will users know this is happening? Is this covered in our current privacy notice?

When teams self-identify privacy considerations, they're already thinking about responsible implementation. Your job becomes much easier when people involve you in planning rather than asking for retroactive approval.

An important Note About Employee Privacy. Employee privacy questions often involve different legal frameworks than customer privacy (employment law, union agreements, state-specific workplace privacy statutes). When HR asks about background checks, performance monitoring, or employee data handling, these typically require Legal input since employment privacy has distinct requirements from customer data privacy. Your role is often to help HR identify when Legal review is needed rather than providing direct guidance on employee privacy matters.

Managing High-Risk Requests

Some requests carry significant privacy risk that requires more careful handling. Have standard approaches ready for scenarios like recording all customer calls "just in case," keeping all employee data "forever for reference," adding invasive tracking "to better understand users," or sharing customer lists with partners without clear agreements.

For high-risk situations, use this framework:

This approach creates significant privacy risk around ________________ [specific concerns].

The potential consequences include ________________ [regulatory exposure, reputational impact].

To proceed responsibly, we'd need ________________ [specific safeguards].

Alternatively, we could explore ________________ [lower-risk options].

This level of risk decision should involve ________________ [Legal/Risk/Senior Leadership].

Field Insight. A privacy colleague used this approach when Product wanted to implement detailed user behavior tracking across their entire application. Instead of just saying "no," she explained: "This level of tracking creates significant privacy risk around user consent and data minimization. The potential consequences include regulatory scrutiny under GDPR and user trust issues. To proceed responsibly, we'd need granular user controls and clear justification for each data point. Alternatively, we could start with anonymous analytics or focus on specific user journeys. This decision should involve senior leadership given the risk profile."

The product team appreciated the clear explanation of trade-offs and worked with her to design a privacy-friendly analytics approach that met their core objectives.

When to Escalate

Know when situations require senior business input beyond your advisory role. Escalate when requests involve sensitive personal data like health, financial, or biometric information, international data transfers to new countries, significant changes to core business practices, potential regulatory reporting requirements, or major vendor relationships.

"Use clear escalation language: This creates material privacy implications that require senior leadership input. The privacy concerns are ______________ [specific issues], the business benefits are ______________ [their case], and the risk decision should be made by ______________ [appropriate authority level]. Should I prepare a brief for ______________ [Legal/Risk/Leadership]?"

When privacy concerns require senior business input, focus on informed decision-making: "I've identified privacy requirements that conflict with the current approach: ______________ [specific issues]. The business objectives are ______________ [their goals]. We have several options: ______________ [compliant alternatives]. This decision involves risk tolerance that should be determined by ______________ [appropriate level of authority]."

For situations involving significant privacy risk, coordinate with Legal to ensure proper decision-making processes and appropriate business ownership of risk decisions.

Building Sustainable Response Patterns

Develop standard approaches for common request types that you can adapt quickly to specific situations.

> **For email marketing:** "We can support email campaigns if we confirm opt-in status and include easy unsubscribe options."

> **For analytics and tracking:** "We can support this tracking if we update our privacy notice and respect user preferences."

> **For vendor integration:** "We can support this integration if they have a current DPA and meet our security requirements."

These patterns help you respond quickly while ensuring consistency in your privacy guidance. Teams start to understand what privacy compliance looks like for their type of work, which reduces the number of basic questions you receive.

Making It Work Long-Term

Follow through consistently. When you set conditions for privacy compliance, help implement them or connect teams with appropriate resources. Your credibility depends on enabling success, not just identifying requirements.

Document decisions and patterns. Track your recommendations and business responses to maintain consistency, demonstrate business enablement, and build institutional knowledge.

Celebrate collaborative wins. When teams involve you early and launch successfully with privacy safeguards, make it visible. This reinforces proactive privacy consultation rather than reactive crisis management.

Build privacy champions. Teams that successfully work with privacy guidance become advocates who refer others and involve privacy in planning rather than implementation.

The Strategic Outcome

Your goal isn't to make business decisions about privacy risk. It's to ensure those decisions are made with full understanding of privacy implications by people with appropriate authority.

When you become known as someone who enables informed decision-making rather than blocking initiatives, teams start involving you in planning rather than seeking post-implementation solutions.

This shift from reactive compliance to proactive consultation is where privacy professionals build lasting influence and create sustainable privacy programs that balance business objectives with privacy protection.

Remember: You provide privacy expertise to inform business decisions. Business leaders make risk decisions based on privacy input alongside other business factors. Your professional responsibility is ensuring decisions are informed, not making the decisions yourself.

PART III:

BUILD THE BACKBONE OF A REAL PROGRAM

In Part II, we focused on traction: proving that privacy can move with the business, handling requests, and building credibility through visible wins. That phase is about momentum, and it is essential. Yet momentum alone is not enough to create something that lasts.

What separates one-off progress from a durable privacy function is structure. A program that endures leadership changes, shifting priorities, and evolving regulations requires a backbone. This backbone does not mean bureaucracy or endless documentation. It means putting the right systems and habits in place so that the work holds its shape over time, even when pressure builds.

The backbone of a real program rests on a few essential elements:

- ☞ Training that people actually internalize rather than ignore.
- ☞ Retention and minimization practices that reduce risk without paralyzing operations.
- ☞ Metrics that matter: evidence that shows progress, demonstrates sustainability, and equips you to defend your work.
- ☞ A minimum viable program framework that provides clarity about how privacy is structured and managed.

None of these elements require perfection. In fact, the pursuit of perfection often undermines programs that could otherwise succeed. The goal is a backbone that is strong enough to provide stability, light enough to adapt, and clear enough that business leaders, regulators, and auditors can see how it works.

This part of the book is about building that backbone piece by piece, so your program evolves from a collection of early wins into something that you can explain, maintain, and defend with confidence.

By the end of this section, you won't just have examples of what privacy work looks like in practice. You'll have the backbone of a program that can carry weight, withstand scrutiny, and grow stronger over time.

CHAPTER 11:

TRAINING THAT PEOPLE DON'T HATE

Ditch the LMS. Train in Context When People Actually Need it

Let's start with an uncomfortable truth: you probably dread the idea of "doing privacy training" almost as much as people dread attending it.

What often goes overlooked is that the most effective privacy training rarely looks like formal training. It happens through practical, solution-oriented conversations with people focused on doing their jobs responsibly.

And you're already doing it.

You're Already Training (And Don't Even Know It)

Every time you help Marketing figure out a campaign consent issue, you're training them. When you walk Product through data minimization for a new feature, that's training too. When Sales asks about sharing prospect data and you help them think through the implications, that's some of the most effective privacy education that will ever happen in your organization.

The difference between privacy training that works and privacy training that doesn't isn't about your presentation skills or training credentials. It's about timing, relevance, and treating people like the capable professionals they are.

Why Traditional Privacy Training Tends to Fail

Most privacy training fails because it violates everything we know about how most of us learn.

It's disconnected from real work. Generic presentations about GDPR principles don't help a product manager figure out how to handle user-generated content or a marketer decide whether they can use a new analytics tool. When training content feels theoretical, people tune out because they can't see how it applies to their immediate challenges.

It tries to cover everything at once. Hour-long sessions that jump from legal frameworks to technical controls to incident response overwhelm people and leave them remembering nothing useful. The human brain can only absorb so much abstract information at once, especially when it's not immediately relevant to current work.

It happens at the wrong time. Annual training delivered in January has little impact on a product launch in September. People forget abstract concepts but remember specific guidance received when they needed it.

It makes people feel limited. Training that emphasizes what people can't do or uses jargon they don't understand creates a "privacy police" dynamic instead of building partnership. When people feel like privacy training is about restrictions rather than enablement, they become defensive rather than engaged.

The Critical Miss

Most critically, traditional training ignores people's professional expertise. We bring years of experience to learning situations. Training that doesn't acknowledge this expertise feels condescending and irrelevant.

The most effective privacy guidance feels like problem-solving with a colleague, not sitting through a lecture about compliance requirements.

When Formal Training Is Required

Before diving into more effective approaches, let's acknowledge the reality: sometimes formal training with employee acknowledgment is genuinely required for compliance purposes.

Standards like HIPAA, NIST Cybersecurity Framework, and SOC 2 often mandate documented training programs where employees must formally acknowledge their understanding of privacy and security policies. These requirements exist for good reasons: they create accountability, demonstrate organizational commitment to compliance, and provide evidence of due diligence during audits.

If your organization needs formal training acknowledgments, you're not exempt from this requirement. But you can still make required training more effective by applying the principles in this chapter. Even mandatory training can be more relevant, timely, and respectful of people's expertise.

The key is distinguishing between training for compliance checkboxes and training for actual behavior change. Do both well, but don't mistake one for the other.

The Mindset Shift: From Training to Conversation

It can be very effective to stop thinking about yourself as a trainer and start thinking about yourself as a helpful colleague who happens to know a lot about privacy.

This shift changes everything about how you approach privacy education:

Instead of delivering content, you're solving problems together. When Marketing asks about a campaign, you're not teaching them email compliance theory. You're helping them launch successfully while protecting customer trust.

Instead of covering predetermined material, you're answering real questions. When Product wonders about data collection for a new feature, you're not explaining abstract privacy-by-design principles. You're helping them build something users will feel good about.

Instead of assessing knowledge retention, you're building practical capability. When Sales needs to understand data sharing rules, you're not testing their memory. You're helping them close deals confidently within appropriate boundaries.

The Goal Shift

The goal isn't making sure people know the rules. It's helping them achieve business objectives through privacy-conscious approaches.

This approach recognizes that adults learn best when they feel respected, supported, and immediately useful.

Just-in-Time Learning That Actually Works

I've seen the most powerful privacy learning happen when people are facing real decisions and genuinely want guidance. These moments create what learning experts call "readiness to learn," when people are motivated to absorb information because they need it right now.

Consider what happens when Marketing is planning a new campaign. They're not thinking about privacy in the abstract. They're thinking about reaching their target audience, driving conversions, and hitting their quarterly goals. They want to know how to achieve these objectives while handling customer data appropriately.

Your role shifts from instructor to consultant. What are they trying to accomplish? What privacy considerations might affect that? How can we make this work while protecting people's information? What would make them feel confident about this approach?

This feels like partnership, not policing. And partnership is where real learning can happen.

The same dynamic applies when Product is designing a feature that collects data, HR is implementing a new recruiting tool, or Sales wants to use lead enrichment services. In each case, people have specific business objectives they want to achieve responsibly. They're ready to learn because the information has immediate utility.

The Three-Minute Rule

Effective privacy guidance can often be delivered in three minutes or less. This isn't because privacy is simple, but because most of us learn best when the information is timely, relevant, and directly tied to the task at hand.

Short video formats are especially effective for this kind of just-in-time learning. Tools like Loom, Vimeo, or internal platforms allow you to record quick walkthroughs that explain a process, clarify a decision, or guide someone through a document. These videos feel conversational, reduce confusion, and eliminate the need for long written instructions or follow-up meetings.

We've seen this approach work well because people can absorb and apply the guidance immediately. It's specific to their situation, not generic. It gives them enough clarity to move forward confidently while positioning you as a helpful partner rather than an obstacle.

You can always follow up with more detail if needed, but most people just need actionable guidance that helps them make a sound decision in the moment.

Success Story: A Quick Video That Changed Team Engagement

In my privacy compliance consulting company, we supported a team working on data subject request workflows, we embedded a Loom video directly in the email alongside three attachments: a Visio diagram of the proposed workflow, a tracking spreadsheet, and a brief compliance scoping document. The video walked through each item and explained how they fit together. The feedback from the team was immediate: they called the format "game changing."

We've applied the same approach to other tasks, like guiding users through a data elements form for a data mapping initiative. A short screen recording with voiceover replaced lengthy written instructions and significantly reduced confusion and rework.

These lightweight videos continue to save time, reduce friction, and make privacy guidance easier to act on.

Embedding Learning in Business Processes

The most sustainable privacy education happens when privacy considerations become part of how people already work, not an additional layer of requirements.

During project planning, instead of requiring separate privacy reviews, build privacy questions into existing planning templates: What personal data will this involve? How will people know we're collecting it? What's our legal basis for this use? How long do we need to keep the data? These questions become natural checkpoints rather than external requirements.

During vendor evaluation, rather than abstract training on third-party risk, provide specific guidance during actual vendor discussions:

> "Here are the key privacy questions for this type of tool. This contract language protects us, this part needs work. Based on our risk tolerance, prioritize these issues."

During campaign development, instead of broad sessions on marketing compliance, offer targeted input during campaign creation:

> "This targeting approach works with our consent model. Here's compliant language for the unsubscribe process. This data source needs additional review."

The Integration Principle

When privacy guidance is embedded in existing workflows, it feels natural rather than burdensome. People get the information they need when they need it, within processes they already understand and use.

Creating Resources People Actually Use

Instead of comprehensive training libraries that sit unused, create a few high-value resources people reference regularly.

A quick decision guide helps people determine when they need privacy input and when they can proceed independently. This simple flowchart reduces unnecessary consultations while ensuring you're involved in genuinely complex decisions.

A common scenario FAQs provides real examples relevant to each team's work, updated based on questions you actually get. This gives people immediate answers to routine questions while documenting your guidance for consistency.

A collection of good examples shows privacy-friendly approaches that achieved business objectives. Screenshots, templates, or case studies demonstrate that privacy protection and business success work together.

Clear contact guidance explains when and how to reach you, including examples of helpful context to include in requests. This makes it easy for people to get the support they need quickly.

Resource Guidelines

Keep these resources brief, visual, and focused on enabling action rather than explaining theory.

Measuring What Matters

Traditional training metrics like completion rates, quiz scores, and hours delivered don't tell you whether people are making better privacy decisions.

Better indicators include behavioral changes like teams proactively involving you in planning, improved quality of privacy questions over time, and self-correction when teams catch potential issues early. These show that people are developing privacy judgment rather than just consuming privacy information.

Relationship indicators matter too. Teams asking for guidance earlier in their processes, positive feedback about privacy support being helpful, and other teams requesting similar guidance after seeing peers benefit all suggest that your approach is working.

Business impact provides the clearest evidence of effective privacy guidance. Reduced compliance issues requiring reactive fixes, faster project approvals due to early privacy consultation, and business initiatives enabled through smart privacy planning demonstrate real value creation.

The Realistic Goal

The goal isn't perfect privacy knowledge across the organization. It's better privacy decision-making by people who understand their role and know when to ask for help.

Practical Next Steps

Whether you're new to privacy education or looking to refine your approach, these strategies can enhance your current efforts.

Look for natural teaching moments in ongoing work – when someone's planning a project, evaluating a vendor, or launching a campaign. Offer brief, specific guidance rather than comprehensive training. Practice the three-minute rule by seeing if you can immediately provide useful guidance quickly and concisely.

Consider building one targeted resource for the team that asks you the most questions. Focus on their most common concerns and provide clear, actionable guidance that builds on what you're already doing.

Most importantly, examine your current role positioning. Whether you're formally designated as a trainer or simply the person people come to with privacy questions, consider how shifting from "privacy trainer" to "privacy consultant" changes the dynamic. The guidance you provide is the same, but the mindset is completely different. You're helping colleagues succeed rather than ensuring they complete training requirements.

CHAPTER 12:

RETENTION AND MINIMIZATION WITHOUT PERFECTION

Pick Your Battles, Start With High-Risk Data, and Build Sustainable Practices

Everyone talks about data minimization and retention, but only few know where to start.

Legal says "keep it all for litigation hold." IT says "storage is cheap, deletion is risky." Marketing says "we might need that data for future campaigns."

So what do most companies do? Nothing. They keep everything, forever.

That's exactly where privacy risk accumulates in forgotten databases, archived folders, and "just in case" collections that no one remembers creating and everyone's afraid to touch.

This chapter is about systematically reducing your data footprint without paralyzing your business or overwhelming your team.

Why This Matters (and Why It's So Hard)

Data minimization isn't optional. GDPR requires personal data be "adequate, relevant and limited to what is necessary," and CPRA requires data collection be "reasonably necessary and proportionate."

But let's be honest about the real risks you're managing. Most organizations aren't facing massive regulatory fines for imperfect retention practices yet. The practical risks are more immediate.

Data subject requests become expensive and time-consuming when you have too much data scattered across systems. Data breaches are more costly and embarrassing when they involve data you didn't need. Storage costs and system performance suffer under the weight of accumulated information. Regulatory inquiries become harder to handle when you can't explain what you have or why you're keeping it.

Here's the truth: data retention and minimization is one of the hardest areas of privacy to get right. Every organization struggles with it. The goal isn't perfection; it's about taking a defensible approach and making steady progress.

Most data minimization efforts fail because they try to solve everything at once instead of starting somewhere manageable. They wait for perfect policies instead of taking practical steps. They frame the work as pure compliance burden instead of business improvement. Most critically, they don't align with Legal from the start, which creates unnecessary friction and risk.

The Essential Legal Partnership

Before implementing any data retention or deletion practices, you must work with Legal to understand applicable requirements. Different industries, jurisdictions, and data types have specific retention obligations that override general privacy principles.

This conversation needs to happen early, not after you've identified problems. Ask Legal about specific retention requirements by data type, how to handle litigation holds and regulatory investigations, and what documentation you need for retention decisions.

For ongoing decisions, establish a clear escalation process. When you find data that's years old and no longer serves its original purpose, you need a quick way to confirm whether legal requirements mandate continued retention.

AI and machine learning present additional complexity around data retention. Regulatory frameworks are still developing around AI training data, algorithmic accountability, and automated decision-making requirements. Legal can help you understand current requirements and anticipate how emerging regulations might affect your retention practices.

Start Where It Matters Most

Work with Legal to identify your highest-risk data categories, then start with one. Choose either your biggest risk or your easiest win.

Forgotten personal data creates the most obvious exposure. Customer records no longer tied to active accounts, prospect data from leads who never converted, and employee data from people who left years ago serve no business purpose but create ongoing compliance obligations.

Sensitive personal data beyond operational necessity represents concentrated risk. Health or financial information that you collected for one purpose but keep for unclear reasons, identity documents stored unnecessarily, and biometric data from discontinued programs all create exposure without corresponding business value.

Unsecured personal data combines data risk with security risk. Personal information in shared drives without access controls, customer data in email attachments, and backup systems with unclear retention and security create multiple vulnerabilities.

Start with one category. Don't try to address everything simultaneously.

Three Phases: Crawl, Walk, Run

Phase 1: Stop the Bleeding

Establish baseline retention periods by working with Legal to understand industry-specific requirements. Customer data retention period might be active relationship plus three years, but your industry might require longer retention. Prospect data might be twelve to twenty-four months post-last engagement. Employee data often needs seven years post-employment, but verify local requirements.

Take immediate action on obviously old data. Archive information that's clearly inactive for two or more years. Configure systems to stop collecting unnecessary data going forward. Document business justification for any extended retention beyond standard periods.

Phase 2: Build Systematic Practices

Create decision frameworks with Legal input. Establish clear criteria for "active" versus "inactive" data and escalation processes for retention decisions involving legal risk. Set regular review cycles for different data types.

Use an archive-first approach when teams are nervous about deletion. Move old data to a secure, separate storage with defined archive retention periods before permanent deletion. This builds confidence and allows you to test your retention decisions on a smaller scale.

Phase 3: Scale and Optimize

Implement graduated retention based on business and legal requirements. Current customers, ongoing matters, and regulatory requirements get longest retention. Recently concluded relationships and completed projects get medium-term retention. Old prospects, expired relationships, and concluded matters get shortest retention.

Handle exceptions systematically by documenting business justification for extended retention, setting specific review dates, and assigning ownership for decisions.

Common Obstacles and Practical Solutions

The "we need to keep everything for litigation" objection comes up constantly. Work with Legal to define what "everything" actually means. Most legal requirements are specific to certain data types and timeframes. You don't need to keep all customer emails forever just because some might be relevant to potential disputes.

The "we might need it someday" concern reflects legitimate business anxiety about losing potentially valuable information. Distinguish between possible need and business necessity. Create archive processes for "might need" data with clear deletion timelines. If you haven't accessed data in three years, you probably don't need it.

The "deletion is too risky" worry is understandable given the irreversible nature of deletion. Start with archiving instead of permanent deletion. Build confidence through smaller, lower-risk decisions before tackling more complex data categories.

When Legal Holds Override Deletion

Sometimes Legal will place a "litigation hold" on data due to actual or anticipated legal proceedings. When this happens, you cannot delete data covered by the hold, even if customers request deletion or your retention schedule says it should be removed.

How to handle this: When you receive deletion requests for data that's under legal hold, coordinate with Legal immediately. Document that the deletion cannot be completed due to legal requirements and inform the data subject that retention is required by law. Once the legal matter concludes and the hold is lifted, you can then process the delayed deletions.

Legal holds take precedence over privacy deletion rights under most privacy laws. Your job is to track these requests and ensure they get processed once the legal constraint is removed. Work with Legal to understand which data categories are affected and for how long, so you can provide realistic timelines to data subjects.

AI Training Data Complexity

Organizations using AI systems face unique retention challenges that traditional data minimization approaches don't address. AI training data often needs to be retained longer than operational data to retrain models, improve performance, or comply with emerging AI regulations. However, some AI systems cannot selectively remove individual records from training datasets without retraining the entire model, which may be technically or economically infeasible.

Work with Legal to understand emerging AI regulations that may require retention of training data for algorithmic accountability, bias testing, or audit purposes. Document what AI systems use personal data for training versus inference, and establish clear policies for when training data can be deleted versus when it must be retained for model integrity.

When individuals request deletion of their data, be transparent about AI system limitations

Measuring Success Practically

Progress indicators show whether your retention practices are working. You should be able to explain what data you have and roughly why you're keeping it. Data subject requests shouldn't require weeks of detective work to fulfill.

Business improvements demonstrate value beyond compliance. Teams should be able to find the data they actually need more easily. System performance should improve as you reduce data bloat. You should spend less time managing and securing data you don't use.

Practical wins show organizational acceptance. Legal should be comfortable with your retention approach. Business teams should see data cleanup as helpful, not obstructive. You should have a process for making retention decisions, even if it's not perfect.

The goal isn't sophisticated measurement. It's demonstrable progress on a genuinely difficult problem that every organization faces.

Moving Forward

The specifics of your data retention approach will depend on your organization's risk profile, regulatory environment, and operational constraints. Some teams find success starting with their highest-risk categories, while others prefer building confidence with easier wins first. The archiving versus deletion decision similarly depends on your team's comfort level and technical capabilities.

Your Legal partnership remains foundational regardless of your starting point. The regulatory landscape around data retention continues to evolve, particularly for AI systems and cross-border data flows. Understanding your specific obligations before implementing changes prevents costly reversals later.

The common thread across successful data minimization efforts is sustained progress rather than perfect execution. Whether you're refining existing practices or building new ones, the goal is meaningful risk reduction through approaches that align with your business operations and legal requirements. Every organization faces these challenges differently, but consistent attention to data lifecycle management compounds into significant risk mitigation over time.

CHAPTER 13:

MONITORING AND METRICS (WITHOUT THE LATEST SOFTWARE)

Track What Matters for Explain, Maintain, and Defend

In my experience, privacy is infrastructure work that needs to run reliably in the background. Your tracking system should demonstrate three things to stakeholders: you're focused on agreed-upon requirements (explain), operations handle required work sustainably (maintain), and you have evidence to prove compliance work was done properly (defend).

I've found that leadership doesn't need sophisticated privacy dashboards. They need confidence that privacy work aligns with organizational priorities and won't create business problems or regulatory exposure.

Why These Three Areas Matter

Explain (Clear Priorities): Shows you're focused on the right things, whether that's regulatory requirements, industry standards, customer trust initiatives, or other defined business objectives. Leadership can see privacy work aligns with organizational priorities.

Maintain (Sustainability): Shows privacy requirements can be handled consistently with available resources and processes. Leadership can see it will keep working even when people change.

Defend (Evidence Collection): Shows you have practical evidence of compliance work completed properly. Leadership can see you can prove what you've done if questioned.

Track Only What Serves These Purposes

Explain Metrics: Are You Focused on Organizational Priorities?

What to track: Work that addresses defined business objectives for privacy

- Regulatory compliance requirements (DSRs, cookie consent, required PIAs)
- Industry standard implementations (healthcare privacy standards, financial services guidelines)
- Customer trust initiatives (privacy certifications, transparency features)
- Board/investor requirements (formal framework compliance)
- Business risk mitigation (vendor assessments, cross-border transfer reviews)

Why track: Proves you're prioritizing actual organizational objectives over theoretical privacy activities

Report as: "Privacy work aligned with business priorities: [X] regulatory items, [X] industry standard items, [X] customer trust initiatives completed within timeframes"

This approach lets you justify privacy work whether it's driven by legal requirements, industry expectations, customer demands, competitive needs, or executive mandates, as long as you can clearly explain why it matters to the organization.

Maintain Metrics:
Is This Sustainable With Available Resources?

What to track: Whether privacy work can continue consistently without overwhelming current capacity

- ☞ Request volume vs. available capacity
- ☞ Process documentation that others can follow
- ☞ Response times remaining stable under normal volume
- ☞ Cross-training and knowledge transfer completion

Why track: Shows whether current approach will keep working when people change or volume grows

Report as: "Privacy work sustainable with current resources: [X] requests handled within capacity, processes documented for continuity"

Defend Metrics:
Do You Have Evidence of Compliance Work?

What to track: Practical proof that compliance work was completed properly

- ☞ Written records of all DSR responses with timestamps
- ☞ Documented vendor assessments with approval rationale
- ☞ Evidence of business consultations with recommendations provided
- ☞ Records of training completion and policy updates

Why track: Creates evidence you can produce if regulators ask "show us what you've done"

Report as: "All compliance work documented with evidence: [X] DSRs with response records, [X] vendor assessments with approval documentation"

Simple Weekly Work Log

Track your work in categories that directly support explain/maintain/defend:

Date	Category	Description	Response Time	Resources Used	Evidence Created
6/15	Explain	DSR processing	25 days	Standard process	Response email with data export
6/14	Maintain	Marketing consultation	Same day	Existing template	Email with consent guidance
6/12	Explain	Vendor GDPR assessment	4 days	Standard checklist	Assessment report with approval
6/10	Defend	Updated vendor template	N/A	Legal basis research	Template with documented changes

Update weekly: 5 minutes to log completed work

Review monthly: Check sustainability and evidence collection

Monthly Reporting Templates

For Your Direct Manager

Subject: Privacy Operations – [Month]

Organizational Priorities: [X] compliance items completed within deadlines. Focus: [specific regulatory/industry/business priority areas].

Sustainability: [X] privacy requirements handled within current capacity. Processes documented for continuity when personnel change.

Evidence Collection (Defend): [X] privacy activities documented with proof of completion. All compliance work has supporting evidence.

Next Month: [One specific improvement that strengthens explain/maintain/defend]

> **Example:** *"Regulatory Compliance: Handled 8 DSRs within CCPA deadlines, completed 3 vendor GDPR assessments. Business Operations: Supported 15 consultations with 1.5-day average response. Process Documentation: All recommendations documented with legal basis, updated vendor template based on Colorado Privacy Act. Next Month: Creating marketing team FAQ to reduce repeat consultations."*

For Legal (When Issues Arise)

Subject: Privacy Items for Legal Review - [Month]

Immediate Legal Input Needed:

- [Specific regulatory interpretation questions]
- [Vendor contracts requiring custom terms]

- [New law changes affecting business processes]

Compliance Items Handled: [Brief summary of regulatory work completed without Legal involvement]

> **Example:** *"Immediate Legal Input: New EU vendor requiring adequacy decision review, Colorado Privacy Act question about employee data. Compliance Items Handled: 6 DSRs, 4 routine vendor assessments, 12 business consultations."*

Red Flags: When to Escalate Immediately

Explain Red Flags (Priority Misalignment)

- **Working on activities without clear business justification:** "Privacy work lacks connection to regulatory requirements, industry standards, or defined business objectives. Need: clarity on organizational privacy priorities."
- **Regulatory deadlines at risk:** "Required compliance work behind schedule. Legal deadlines for _________________ [specific requirement] at risk."
- **Business priorities unclear:** "Multiple stakeholders requesting different privacy focuses. Need: leadership clarity on privacy program priorities."

Maintain Red Flags (Sustainability Risk)

- **Request volume exceeding documented capacity:** "Privacy request volume exceeding sustainable capacity. Current resources can handle [X] monthly. Above that: delays or quality issues."

- ☞ **Processes dependent on single person:** "Privacy work depends on individual knowledge rather than documented processes. Risk: program failure if personnel change."
- ☞ **No cross-training or knowledge transfer:** "Privacy knowledge concentrated in one person. Need: documentation and training to ensure continuity."

Defend Red Flags (Evidence Gaps)

- ☞ **Compliance work completed without documentation:** "Privacy work completed but lacking evidence for regulatory review. Need: ________________ [specific documentation process]."
- ☞ **Inconsistent evidence collection:** "Some privacy activities documented, others not. Need: ________________ [standardization] to ensure all compliance work has supporting evidence."

Use Your Tracking for Resource Requests

When you need additional capacity, your explain/maintain/defend data makes compelling business cases:

Resource Request Formula

Current Explain Capability: "Privacy program addresses [specific organizational priorities: regulatory/industry/business objectives] through documented processes. [X]% of privacy work aligns with defined priorities."

Current Maintain Capability: "Privacy operations handle [X] monthly requirements with documented processes. Sustainable with current resources and transferable to other personnel."

Current Defend Capability: "[X]% of privacy work documented with evidence. Ready to show regulators proof of compliance activities."

Capacity Limit: "Above [specific threshold], we cannot maintain [explain/maintain/defend standard]. Risk: [specific compliance impact]."

Resource Solution: "[Specific resource] enables [specific improvement] while maintaining explain/maintain/defend standards at [higher volume]."

> **Example:** *"Privacy program ensures CCPA/GDPR compliance through documented processes, 95% response rate within legal deadlines. Operations handle 40 monthly requests without business delays, 2-day average response. 90% of decisions documented with clear rationale. Above 60 monthly requests, cannot maintain 2-day response times. Risk: business operations delayed, regulatory deadlines at risk. Privacy automation software maintains current standards at 80+ monthly requests."*

Getting Started This Week

Day 1: Set Up Tracking

- ☞ Create work log template
- ☞ Decide where you'll track (spreadsheet, shared doc, simple tool)
- ☞ Start logging work as explain/maintain/defend categories

Week 4: First Monthly Report

- ☞ Calculate explain/maintain/defend metrics from your log
- ☞ Send monthly update to your manager
- ☞ Note one improvement for next month

Month 3: Establish Baseline

- Review whether you can confidently answer explain/maintain/defend questions
- Send quarterly summary if appropriate
- Adjust processes based on patterns

What Success Looks Like After 6 Months

Explain: "We focus on defined organizational priorities. [X]% of our work addresses specific regulatory requirements, industry standards, or business objectives we can clearly justify."

Maintain: "Privacy operations handle required work sustainably. We complete [X] requirements monthly with documented processes that can continue when personnel change."

Defend: "All privacy work creates evidence. We can show regulators documentation of [X] completed activities with proof of proper completion."

This tracking approach shouldn't take more than 10–15 minutes weekly but creates the foundation for demonstrating competent privacy management that leadership can confidently explain to auditors, investors, or regulators.

The goal isn't sophisticated measurement. It's organized evidence that your privacy work follows a systematic approach focused on regulatory compliance, operational sustainability, and defensible decision-making.

CHAPTER 14:

THE MINIMUM VIABLE PRIVACY PROGRAM

Structure What You've Built into Something You Can Explain and Defend

You've been tracking your privacy work systematically. You know what you're doing and why. But when leadership asks, "How's our privacy program?" you need to present your work as a coherent system, not just a collection of activities.

In my experience, you already have a privacy program. You just need to organize it clearly using the explain/maintain/defend framework that I've seen work consistently across different organizations.

Why Start Simple

Complex frameworks like NIST Privacy Framework, ISO 27701, or comprehensive accountability models like the ICO Accountability Framework might not be necessary for every organization. Those are generally designed for mature organizations with dedicated teams and more complex needs.

What works better for most organizations is something you can explain quickly to anyone who asks, maintain without overwhelming your workload, and defend confidently in any conversation about privacy.

Many privacy professionals make the mistake of trying to build comprehensive frameworks before they've mastered the basics. This creates impressive documentation that nobody uses and complex processes that break under pressure.

Organize Around Explain, Maintain, Defend

Your privacy program needs to demonstrate three capabilities clearly:

Explain: We focus on defined organizational priorities and can justify every privacy activity with specific regulatory requirements, industry standards, or business objectives

Maintain: We handle privacy requirements sustainably with available resources and documented processes that continue when people change

Defend: We collect evidence of compliance work that we can produce if questioned

Everything else is optional until your organization's complexity requires additional sophistication.

Two Simple Tools to Present Your Program

Tool 1: Privacy Program Charter (Your Reference Document)

A one-page charter explaining your program's approach to anyone who asks. Update it annually or when core processes change.

Sample Privacy Program Charter

ACME Corp Privacy Program Charter

Privacy Contact: [Your name and role]

Email: privacy@company.com | Response commitment: 24 hours initial response, 48 hours for guidance

How We Explain Our Approach:

- All privacy activities address specific organizational priorities: regulatory requirements (GDPR, CCPA), industry standards, or defined business objectives
- Business consultations focus on applicable compliance obligations and industry best practices
- Vendor assessments target regulatory compliance and industry standard gaps
- AI systems reviewed for regulatory requirements and industry transparency standards

How We Maintain Sustainability:

- Privacy work handled within available resource capacity
- All processes documented so others can perform the work
- Response times sustainable without overtime or heroic effort

- Knowledge transfer procedures ensure continuity when personnel change

How We Defend With Evidence:

- All DSR responses documented with timestamps and completion records
- Vendor assessments documented with approval/rejection rationale
- Business consultations recorded with written recommendations
- Training completion records and policy update evidence maintained

Team Resources:

- Privacy assessment templates: [location]
- Vendor review checklist: [location]
- Training materials: [location]
- DSR portal: [location]

Tool 2: Monthly Privacy Program Dashboard

A simple dashboard showing current performance and demonstrating systematic capability. Update monthly using your tracking data from Chapter 10.

Sample Monthly Dashboard

ACME Corp Privacy Program – [Month] 2025

Explain Performance:

- Organizational priorities addressed: [X] regulatory items, [X] industry standard items, [X] business objective items completed
- Focus areas this month: [specific regulatory/industry/business priority work]
- Priority alignment: [X]% of privacy work addresses defined organizational objectives

Maintain Performance:

- Resource sustainability: [X] requirements handled within available capacity
- Process documentation: [X]% of privacy work follows documented procedures
- Knowledge transfer: [training completed/documentation updated/cross-training status]

Defend Performance:

- Evidence collected: [X]% of compliance work documented with proof
- Records maintained: DSR responses, vendor approvals, consultation records
- Audit readiness: [evidence available/gaps identified]

Next Month Priorities:

- [One regulatory focus area]
- [One operational improvement]
- [One documentation/process enhancement]

Present Results, Not Just Activities

Frame your privacy work in terms of business-relevant outcomes that support explain/maintain/defend:

Instead of Activity Language:

- "Processed 12 DSRs last month"
- "Reviewed 4 vendor contracts"
- "Conducted 3 training sessions"
- "Completed 2 privacy assessments"

Use Results Language:

- **Explain:** "Ensured 100% compliance with data subject request deadlines and implemented industry standard consent management practices."
- **Maintain:** "Privacy requirements handled sustainably: vendor reviews completed using documented processes that any trained team member can follow."
- **Defend:** "Privacy training completed for 45 employees with documented completion records and evidence of required privacy knowledge transfer."

This language shows the business value of systematic privacy management rather than just listing completed tasks.

Respond Confidently to "More Comprehensive" Questions

Eventually, someone will ask whether you need formal privacy frameworks, maturity assessments, or comprehensive coverage models. These questions often come from board members, auditors, or stakeholders expecting specific compliance standards.

Your confident response framework:

"Can we explain our privacy approach?"
"Yes. Our privacy program addresses specific regulatory requirements through documented processes. Every privacy activity maps to legal obligations we can cite."

"Can we maintain this as we grow?"
"Yes. Privacy requirements are handled efficiently without creating business bottlenecks. We complete required work within reasonable timeframes."

"Can we defend our approach?"
"Yes. All compliance work creates evidence we can produce if questioned. We have documentation showing what we've done and when we did it."

If they want more sophistication: *"Our current approach covers regulatory requirements effectively. We can add formal frameworks when business complexity justifies additional structure, but our foundation handles current needs reliably."*

Monthly Stakeholder Communication

Keep stakeholders informed with brief updates using your dashboard data:

For Business Leadership (Quarterly)

Subject: Privacy Program Performance – [Quarter]

Bottom Line: Privacy program operating effectively. Regulatory compliance maintained, business operations supported, systematic decision-making documented.

Explain Status: [X]% of privacy work addresses defined organizational priorities (regulatory, industry standards, business objectives). Current focus: [priority area].

Maintain Status: Privacy work handled sustainably within available resources. Processes documented for continuity when personnel change.

Defend Status: [X]% of compliance activities documented with evidence. Can produce records showing proper completion of privacy work.

Business Impact: [Specific example of how privacy work prevented problems or enabled business outcomes]

Resource Status: Current approach sustainable / Need: [specific resource for specific reason]

For Your Direct Manager (Monthly)

Subject: Privacy Operations Update – [Month]

Regulatory Work: [X] compliance items completed within deadlines. Focus: [specific regulatory area].

Business Support: [X] consultations completed, [average response time]. Teams getting privacy guidance without delays.

Documentation: All recommendations documented with clear rationale. Process improvement: [specific example].

Next Month: [One area of focus that strengthens explain/maintain/defend]

Implementation: Next 30 Days

Week 1: Create Your Charter

1. Draft your one-page privacy program charter using the template I shared above
2. Focus on explaining your current approach using explain/maintain/defend framework
3. Share with your manager for feedback

Week 2: Organize Your Evidence

4. Compile examples of regulatory work (explain)
5. Gather performance data from your tracking (maintain)
6. Organize documentation showing systematic decisions (defend)

Week 3: Test Your Explanation

7. Practice explaining your privacy program in 2 minutes to executives
8. Practice a 5-minute version for business partners
9. Practice a 15-minute detailed version for auditors/stakeholders

Week 4: Launch Regular Communication

10. Send the first monthly update using the dashboard template
11. Schedule quarterly updates for appropriate leadership
12. Refine based on feedback

What You Can Confidently Say

After implementing this minimum viable approach, you can confidently answer:

"Do we have a privacy program?"
"Yes. We have systematic processes for regulatory compliance, business support, and decision documentation that we can explain to anyone."

"How do we know it's working?"
"We track performance monthly and can show consistent regulatory compliance, sustainable operations, and documented decision-making."

"Are we ready for regulatory scrutiny?"
"Yes. All privacy decisions follow documented standards with clear legal rationale. We have systematic evidence of our compliance approach."

"Can this scale with business growth?"
"Yes. We track capacity and performance monthly. Current processes are sustainable and we know exactly when additional resources would be needed."

Building on This Foundation

This minimum viable approach creates the foundation for more sophisticated privacy management when business needs justify additional complexity.

In my experience, most organizations don't need formal frameworks immediately. Your explain/maintain/defend foundation should handle most privacy requirements effectively while remaining maintainable and defensible.

However, eventually someone might ask whether you need formal privacy frameworks, maturity assessments, or comprehensive coverage models. These questions often come from board members, auditors, investors, or stakeholders expecting specific compliance standards.

When that happens, you can build confidently on your foundation:

- **Formal frameworks** (NIST Privacy Framework, ISO 27701, ICO Accountability Framework) can build on your explain/maintain/defend foundation rather than replacing it
- **Maturity assessments** can measure against your systematic approach to organizational priorities
- **Advanced automation** can scale your documented processes and evidence collection
- **Comprehensive audits** can validate your systematic approach to priority alignment

Your confident response: *"Our current approach covers privacy requirements effectively through explain/maintain/defend principles. We can add formal frameworks when business complexity or stakeholder requirements justify additional structure, but our foundation handles current needs reliably."*

The goal is to demonstrate competent privacy management through clear organization of systematic work, not impressive documentation that nobody uses or complex processes that break under pressure.

Complex frameworks aren't necessarily wrong; they work best for mature organizations with dedicated teams and complex needs. Your leadership might mandate formal frameworks for external reasons: board requirements, investor expectations, regulatory guidance, or industry standards. When that happens, you can implement formal frameworks on top of your existing foundation rather than starting over. Your explain/maintain/defend approach provides the operational capability that makes comprehensive frameworks actually work instead of becoming compliance theater.

Start with your charter and dashboard. Most privacy programs need clear organization of good work more than they need sophisticated frameworks or comprehensive coverage assessments.

CHAPTER 15:

WHEN TO INVEST IN PRIVACY TECHNOLOGY

Build the Foundation First

Privacy technology is more advanced than ever. Today's tools can discover personal data across sprawling systems, automate subject request fulfillment, detect risky vendor terms, and even apply AI to streamline reviews. But these capabilities only deliver results when the organization is ready to absorb them.

That readiness rarely exists at the start.

Many companies rush to invest in technology expecting automation to replace effort. What they find instead is stalled implementations, frustrated stakeholders, and underused platforms. Even privacy officers with strong strategic vision get caught in the gap between what was sold in a demo and what's feasible to execute without solid foundations.

Even privacy tech vendors (frustrated by non-renewals of expensive software) now admit that companies should wait to adopt most tools until their privacy program is structurally in place. Without defined workflows, accountable owners, and operational clarity, tools designed to streamline end up amplifying chaos.

Essential Infrastructure vs. Operational Enhancement

Some tools need to come early, especially when technical enforcement is mandated.

- **Consent management platforms (CMPs)** and **cookie control tools** are largely essential for public websites. They enable you to stop non-essential tracking until choices are made and handle jurisdictional requirements. No organization can scale manual enforcement here.
- **Basic scanning tools** help you monitor website changes and compliance, especially when marketing or product teams frequently launch new content or tags.

These are the exceptions.

Most other privacy technologies, from subject rights automation to vendor risk platforms to AI-driven data discovery, function best when your program already works manually.

Why Automated Doesn't Mean Effortless

Yes, some tools claim to auto-discover personal data or apply machine learning to identify risks. That's partially true. But effective deployment requires significant IT and security coordination, stakeholder buy-in, and ongoing human configuration. Rules must be tailored. Results must be validated. Outputs must be triaged and acted upon. When those foundational pieces don't exist, the tools either produce overwhelming noise or sit unused. The investment becomes a sunk cost.

The Readiness Assessment

You're ready to invest in privacy tech when:

- **Accountability is clear.** Someone owns privacy outcomes and has the authority to drive tech implementation.
- **You know what "good" looks like.** You can articulate success criteria and configure technology to match your context.
- **You understand current workflows.** You can design automation that fits the way decisions are made and how work gets done.
- **Ongoing coordination is covered.** Someone is responsible for maintaining the tool and coordinating its use across teams. This can be a dedicated internal lead or outsourced privacy admin support. Without clear ownership, the technology will degrade and eventually fail.

If you can't answer these questions, technology is likely to create more confusion than value.

Common Pitfalls to Avoid

- **Buying too early.** Large platforms offer breadth, but they require mature teams to configure and sustain. Most organizations use a fraction of what they pay for.
- **Automating broken processes.** If your DSR flow is inconsistent and unclear, automation will make it consistently unclear.
- **Underestimating effort.** Every tool needs maintenance, training, updates, and alignment with business realities.
- **Expecting tools to drive alignment.** Collaboration, accountability, and program structure must precede technology. Not follow it.

Smart Technology Choices

When you are ready, start small. Choose one tool to solve one problem you already understand. Look for:

- A clear pain point that tech can measurably reduce
- A defined process that the tool can enhance, not invent
- An internal owner who will maintain the platform and train others

Then expand. Let technology scale what you've already built.

Technology as a Force Multiplier

The groundwork matters. Clarified ownership, streamlined requests, reliable workflows, and accurate maps of your activities are what turn technology into a multiplier, not a liability.

When privacy tech lands in a well-run program, it enhances. When it lands in chaos, it adds cost and confusion.

The Cost of Getting This Wrong. Organizations that invest in privacy technology before building operational foundations typically see most platform capabilities go unused, require expensive customization to fit broken processes, and often revert to manual workarounds within 18 months. The technology becomes shelfware while the underlying problems persist.

PART IV:

PRIVACY LEADERSHIP, NOT PERFECTION

Parts I through III focused on the real-world work of privacy: mapping activities, fixing broken processes and building workflows that actually run. Along the way, we addressed automation, AI, and tooling, where they help, and where they don't.

This section shifts the focus to what sustains that work over time: **credibility, influence, and resilience.**

Even with better tools and maturing infrastructure, privacy programs don't succeed because a platform flagged the right risk. They succeed because someone followed up, explained it, got buy-in, and made the fix stick. That part of the work doesn't come from software. It comes from people who know how to lead.

This section is about that leadership.

- What it looks like when you're the only one asking privacy questions in a product meeting.
- How to build influence across teams with other priorities.
- How to sustain energy when your work is invisible, or hard to quantify.
- And how to create change that lasts, without burning out.

Because privacy leadership isn't about perfection. It's about showing up consistently and helping the business explain, sustain and defend the privacy compliance initiatives they have supported

CHAPTER 16:

HOW TO BUILD INFLUENCE WITHOUT AUTHORITY

Making Privacy Work Across Contexts, Teams, and Time

By this stage in your privacy work, you have likely built credibility. You are brought into the right conversations, trusted to handle reviews, and relied upon to answer nuanced questions. But the influence that works when responding to a single privacy request does not automatically scale when you need to shape privacy culture, guide cross-functional decisions, or support enterprise-wide priorities.

This chapter explores how to build influence when formal authority is limited. Influence, in this context, is not about charisma or persuasion. It is about trust, timing, context awareness, and the ability to create meaningful momentum. It is a leadership skill, not a personality trait. And in privacy, it is indispensable.

Start with Trust, Not Authority

Trust is the cornerstone of influence in privacy work. Without it, even sound recommendations will stall. With it, informal nudges can shape large decisions. But trust is not generic. There are three forms you need to build:

- **Credibility**: Do people believe you understand the subject matter and their environment?
- **Reliability**: Do you follow through, meet deadlines, and show consistency?
- **Intent**: Do stakeholders believe you are acting in the best interest of the organization rather than for personal gain?

In smaller organizations, this often grows through repeated, practical interactions. In larger environments, it requires visible contributions that align with strategic priorities.

> **Field Insight**: One privacy lead gained trust with engineering not by lecturing on legal requirements but by helping reduce review cycles during sprint planning. This showed an understanding of development cadence while embedding risk controls.

If you are struggling to gain traction, examine which element of trust might be missing. The issue may not be your message, but how it is received.

Context Is Your Leverage Point

The most common reason privacy advice is ignored is almost always misalignment with how the organization actually works. Influence is contextual. What matters most is not just what you say, but how well your approach aligns with how people make decisions, what they prioritize, and which internal narratives they trust.

You do not need to control the decision; you need to shape the context in which it is made.

This means listening before proposing, observing which terms resonate, understanding decision cycles, and identifying who drives momentum.

Field Insight: A global privacy program embedded consent guidance into an AI governance rollout because the AI initiative already had executive attention. Privacy did not lead. It accelerated what mattered to the business and in doing so gained long-term support.

Build Coalitions Before You Need Them

Many privacy professionals try to push through an initiative and only realize too late that they are missing allies. The most successful programs are socialized before they are formalized. This requires building coalitions that span functions, levels, and priorities.

There are three categories of stakeholders to consider:

- **Champions**: People who advocate for privacy because they see its value
- **Gatekeepers**: Stakeholders who can block or delay your work, such as legal, procurement, and finance
- **Operators**: The teams doing the daily work, who will absorb the burden of privacy if it is poorly implemented

Each of these groups responds to different forms of influence. Champions need vision. Gatekeepers need clarity and alignment. Operators need usability.

> **Field Insight**: A privacy team secured long-term adoption of their request-handling playbook by first piloting it with one frontline team, documenting improvements in turnaround time, and then inviting feedback from skeptical managers. Early visibility built credibility that made later adoption easier.

Privacy wins do not come from corner offices alone. They come from distributed buy-in across the system, and that buy-in comes from relationships, not requests.

Stakeholder Influence Map: A Practical Tool

To apply these principles, it helps to visualize your stakeholder landscape. A simple influence map allows you to assess not just who is involved, but how to tailor your approach based on their position and current mindset.

Try the grid below to organize stakeholders along two dimensions to see if they can help you:

- **Level of Influence**: How much they can shape outcomes, directly or indirectly
- **Level of Support**: How aligned they are (today) with the privacy initiative or direction

This tool is especially useful during a project's early stages or when privacy maturity varies across functions.

Sample Map:
Preparing for a Company-Wide Consent Experience Redesign

	High Influence	**Low Influence**
High Support	**Strategic Allies**	**Friendly Contributors**
	General Counsel: Wants to modernize risk posture across web assets	HR Manager: Values internal transparency and volunteered as a tester
	Head of Product: Sees consent UX as aligned with roadmap simplification goals	Junior Engineer: Pointed out technical debt in legacy cookie banners
Low Support	**Persuadable Priorities**	**Monitor and Inform**
	VP of Marketing: Concerned about friction in lead capture	Regional Sales Lead: Not opposed, but focused on revenue pressures
	Digital Experience Director: Focused on A/B testing speed, not privacy layers	

How to Use the Map

Strategic Allies should be engaged early to co-create and co-sponsor messaging, timelines, and solutions. Their support will open doors and clear obstacles.

Persuadable Priorities require more listening. Meet them where they are. Frame your approach in terms of what they are already trying to accomplish.

Friendly Contributors may not move budgets, but they offer insights and social proof. Involve them in early demos, documentation pilots, or training feedback.

Monitor and Inform stakeholders should be kept in the loop. Do not push for full engagement unless their position changes.

Field Insight: In this example, reframing the initiative as "simplifying consent experiences to reduce page load and complaints" shifted the Digital Experience Director's posture from passive resistance to cautious interest. Privacy was no longer positioned as a compliance burden but as an improvement to overall UX quality.

Behind the Tool

This influence map is adapted from widely used models in organizational change, stakeholder management, and consulting frameworks. It draws from the structure of power-support grids used by firms like McKinsey, behavioral models from Kotter's change leadership principles, and applied stakeholder tiering practices from privacy program consulting. The example provided here reflects real-world patterns observed across privacy engagements, reinterpreted specifically for operational use in data governance, marketing, product, and legal teams.

Its purpose is not academic. It is a practical tool for deciding where to focus your influence, who to engage early, and how to bring others into your work as advocates.

Use Momentum, Not Resistance

Trying to convince others to prioritize privacy on your timeline rarely works. A more effective approach is to align privacy to initiatives that are already in motion. This may include product releases, regulatory audits, data governance efforts, or digital transformation programs.

Rather than competing for attention, attach to what already has visibility. This is not reactive; it is strategic.

Field Insight: A privacy leader at a retail chain used the rollout of a customer loyalty revamp to introduce better consent management because the loyalty team already needed a UX overhaul. The privacy layer became a value-add rather than a roadblock.

This requires keeping a wide-angle view of the business. Know who is launching what, when budget decisions are being made, and what metrics are drawing attention from leadership. Influence often comes from timing, not force.

Make It Easy to Say Yes

As privacy professionals, we sometimes make the right thing hard to do. Dense language, long workflows, and unclear steps create barriers to collaboration. Influence grows when your guidance feels like enablement, not enforcement.

Ask yourself:

- ☞ Can the person act on this guidance today without needing another meeting?
- ☞ Is the risk framed in a way they understand and care about?
- ☞ Have I removed the friction that would cause delay or avoidance?

Field Insight: A company embedded two privacy prompts into its product launch playbook after realizing teams avoided the standalone review form. The change increased visibility into sensitive features without adding a separate workflow.

Simplification is not a compromise. It is a skill. Make it easier for others to do privacy well, and they will include you earlier and more often.

Tell Better Stories

Data helps, but stories move people. Privacy is often positioned internally alongside IT, security, or procurement, not as a driver of growth, but as a foundation for operational integrity. To build influence, it can help to speak the language of real outcomes.

When advocating for your work, emphasize how privacy reduces rework, avoids costly missteps, secures funding by keeping compliance clean, or prevents late-stage blockers and reputational damage. Use examples that make the cost of *not* addressing privacy visible.

Instead of saying, "We need to conduct a DPIA," try:
"We should take a moment to consider whether this use of data might raise questions from regulators or stall legal approval later. It is faster to flag it now than to unwind it later."

Framing privacy in terms of risk reduction, readiness, and business continuity builds credibility and gets attention, without overselling it as a strategic differentiator. Influence grows when privacy is seen as operationally smart, not aspirational.

Case studies, especially internal ones, help normalize good practices. Share stories of collaboration, not just enforcement. Highlight business partners who helped improve a process, reduce risk, or ship something cleaner.

You are not just building awareness. You are reinforcing a story about what privacy success looks like.

Influence Is a System You Build

Sustainable influence is operational. It is not about convincing people once. It is about embedding privacy into how the organization works, so your influence continues even when you are not present.

This includes:

- Designing processes that prompt privacy reviews at the right time
- Embedding controls into systems, not separate from them
- Creating templates and toolkits that support decentralized decisions
- Training others to handle common scenarios without escalation

---

Field Insight: A hospitality group created a standardized vendor intake workflow embedded into procurement systems. This reduced privacy review time by 40 percent while maintaining oversight. The process improvement gave the privacy team more space to focus on strategic issues.

When others carry privacy forward without needing your intervention, that is influence working at scale.

Lead Without Needing Credit

Privacy leadership often happens quietly. You may not get recognition in the executive town hall. But if your work shows up in the decisions made, the systems implemented, and the relationships strengthened, it is working.

The strongest privacy programs are not built on authority. They are built on reliable relationships, timing, relevance, and repeatable practice.

CHAPTER 17:

WHEN YOU'RE THE ONLY ONE WHO CARES

How to Sustain Your Energy When Privacy Feels Like a Solo Mission

Some days, it feels like you're the only person in your company who thinks privacy matters.

Marketing wants to maximize data reach. Sales talks about leveraging every customer touchpoint. Product teams chase frictionless user experiences. And you're the one asking uncomfortable questions: "Do we have consent for this?" "What's our legal basis?" "How long are we retaining this data?"

You get blank stares, polite deflection, or worse, silence. And after a while, you start to question yourself. Are you overthinking it? Is privacy really as critical as you believe?

If that sounds familiar, you're not alone. Nearly every privacy professional goes through moments, sometimes long stretches, of feeling like the only one carrying the weight of this work.

This chapter is about how to stay grounded, build influence, and sustain momentum when it feels like no one else is paying attention.

Why This Feeling Is Common (and Not a Sign of Failure)

Privacy roles are structurally isolating. Unlike other functions, you are often not connected to a large team or department. You span multiple business units but rarely own any of them. You make recommendations, but you do not usually control decisions. And most importantly, when privacy is working well, it is invisible.

No one notices the marketing campaign that did not result in a complaint. Or the vendor risk you quietly eliminated. Or the DSR workflow that prevented a backlog. Privacy success is often the absence of disaster, not the presence of celebration.

You are also operating with a different urgency. While other teams work toward concrete deadlines like product launches, quarterly targets and campaign metrics, privacy risk often remains theoretical until it becomes painfully real. This makes it easy to deprioritize.

And unlike security, which now enjoys broader institutional backing, privacy is still emerging as a formal discipline in many organizations. The result is that you are asking people to slow down in a culture that rewards speed, and asking them to care about a risk they cannot see.

Understanding this context helps. It reminds you that the isolation is structural, not personal and that it can be addressed strategically.

Diagnosing What Kind of Resistance You're Facing

When you feel alone, it helps to get specific about why. Not all resistance is the same, and each type calls for a different response.

Here's a practical reference you can use to interpret common signals:

What They Say	**What It Really Means**	**How to Respond**
"Privacy laws don't apply to us."	Lack of understanding	Educate with peer examples. Avoid theory; use specifics.
"We can't delay the launch."	Time or resource pressure	Offer lightweight solutions that fit existing workflows.
"Revenue comes first."	Misaligned incentives	Connect privacy to risk avoidance or efficiency gains.
"We've always done it this way."	Habitual behavior, not malice	Demonstrate a better alternative. Show, don't argue.

Field Insight: In one company, a marketing lead kept brushing off cookie banner concerns until a competing firm faced a regulator fine for the same issue. Framing it as "proactive cleanup" rather than "legal compliance" shifted the tone of the conversation and won internal support.

If you can understand what kind of resistance you're dealing with, you can choose your battles, tailor your message, and avoid burning energy on the wrong fights.

Finding Support You Didn't Know You Had

Even when no one has "privacy" in their job title, you are likely not alone. The key is identifying privacy-adjacent allies and slowly drawing them into your orbit.

Start with people who already think in adjacent terms:

- The security lead who cares about system integrity
- The engineer who prefers clean, well-documented data
- The product manager who worries about customer trust
- The marketer who focuses on relationship-based growth
- The procurement or finance partner who wants vendor risk off their plate

These allies may not be waving privacy flags, but they are often receptive to privacy conversations when framed in terms they already care about.

Build these relationships over time. Ask what problems they're solving. Then look for small ways privacy can help, not by adding friction, but by clarifying or simplifying a decision they are already facing.

Low-Effort Moves That Build Credibility Over Time

When you feel invisible or unsupported, the temptation is to go quiet or only speak when something goes wrong. But this is the time to be visible in small, strategic ways.

- Create a one-page explainer about a new privacy requirement for a team launching a product
- Offer to pilot a lightweight privacy checklist with a single team, not the whole organization
- Share an example of a peer company's privacy misstep, especially when it shows what not to do
- Use moments of opportunity like AI reviews, vendor onboarding, or retention audits, to make privacy feel useful rather than obstructive
  You do not need permission to create visibility. You just need to stay useful.

Field Insight: A privacy lead in a tech company started including "privacy insights" at the end of monthly security newsletters. Within two quarters, product managers began reaching out before launch, not because they were told to, but because they saw privacy as part of a broader risk-aware culture.

Turning Personal Experience Into Influence

When formal influence is limited, personal experience is one of your best assets. Most people have felt their privacy compromised, not in theory, but in practice. Maybe they noticed their phone listening in, got ads for something they only talked about, or struggled to unsubscribe from a marketing list.

Use these shared moments to bridge the gap between abstract compliance and real impact. Not to provoke fear, but to ground the conversation in human experience.

- ☞ "You know that moment when you get a retargeting ad *before* you even finish the signup flow? That's what we're trying to avoid with better cookie timing and tag firing."
- ☞ "Think about how frustrating it is to email 'unsubscribe' and still get follow-ups. That's what our suppression list and opt-out logic needs to prevent."
- ☞ "It's like when you call customer service and they ask for your name five times. That's why we care about data minimization and system handoffs."

When people connect emotionally, even briefly, they begin to care structurally. Personal experience becomes a lever for influencing decisions, even when authority is limited.

What to Do When You Need a Break

It's okay to step back. Carrying the privacy mindset in an organization that isn't ready can be emotionally depleting. If your efforts are not landing, redirect your focus for a while.

- ☞ Build your skills – take a course, attend a webinar, dive deeper into tech or law
- ☞ Contribute to the external privacy community – sometimes validation comes from peers, not your organization
- ☞ Pick one improvement that is fully in your control and quietly do it well

Progress is not always external. Sometimes, sustaining your clarity and sharpening your tools is the work.

Signs You're Gaining Influence (Even If It Doesn't Feel Like It Yet)

- Someone you have never met forwards you a privacy question
- A product manager asks for input before launch instead of after
- A marketing colleague repeats something you explained about consent
- Legal invites you to a meeting instead of summarizing it for you
- A team references your checklist or template without being prompted
- You are asked to weigh in on something outside of privacy, because they trust your judgment
- A past critic becomes a regular point of contact

Influence does not always arrive with a title or recognition. Sometimes it shows up in small behavioral changes that reflect your impact.

You Are Ahead of the Curve

Privacy will not always feel like this. The regulatory landscape is changing. Customer expectations are shifting. The pressure will come but you do not have to wait for it to start acting like a leader.

Keep your standards high, your tone constructive, and your presence consistent.

You're not behind; you're early. You're not unsupported; you're building the support network that will become the foundation later.

CHAPTER 18:

TROUBLESHOOTING WHEN THINGS GO WRONG

Quick Recovery Moves for Common Privacy Program Failures

Even well-built privacy programs hit snags. The difference between privacy professionals who thrive and those who struggle isn't whether they encounter problems. It's how quickly they recover when things inevitably go wrong.

Most privacy failures follow predictable patterns. Recognizing these patterns early lets you respond before issues escalate into full-blown crises.

Not All Privacy Problems Are Your Problems. Data breach response and crisis communications are typically managed by IT Security teams in coordination with Legal and PR. Privacy professionals may support with context or data flow analysis but are rarely the lead in active incident response. Focus your energy where it matters most.

When Your Processes Break Down

Privacy programs rely on coordinated workflows that span departments and systems. When these break, they tend to fail visibly and painfully.

The DSR Death Spiral

The warning signs are unmistakable:

- Data subject requests start piling up
- Response times lag
- Responses become inconsistent or incomplete

The underlying cause is often scale. What worked at five requests per month collapses under the weight of twenty. But not all spirals start with volume. Sometimes, one broken workflow or a single dead link in a confirmation email quietly derails the entire process. By the time you notice, the backlog is already growing.

Practical Fix

- Triage requests by urgency and complexity
- Streamline the current workflow to manage immediate volume
- Communicate realistic expectations: "You can expect your request to be completed by [date]"

Root causes typically include:

- Inconsistent criteria for what to include in responses
- Lack of reusable templates
- Unclear ownership across systems
- Broken automation, outdated links, or incorrect routing rules

Fix these systematically, not all at once. One reliable fix, implemented well, is better than five half-baked patches.

The Vendor Review Bottleneck

You'll know this is happening when:

- Teams start bypassing the review process
- People ask to "skip privacy just this once"
- Executives question the value added

But it's not always resistance, it's often delay. If privacy is perceived as unpredictable or slow, teams will move without it.

Practical Fix

- Use tiered reviews: fast-track low-risk vendors, apply full diligence to higher-risk ones
- Publish clear timelines and criteria for each level
- Define what qualifies as "low risk" and keep that list visible
- Build in intake questions that route reviews automatically to the right track
- Offer a self-serve privacy FAQ or checklist for simple tools

Most bottlenecks stem from a one-size-fits-all process or from unclear ownership. Match effort to risk, and make the path visible from the start.

When Relationships Go Sideways

Becoming the Privacy Police

If teams avoid you, delay engagement, or treat privacy as a barrier, it may signal that your role is seen as punitive. This often happens when privacy is introduced late, framed in absolutes, or perceived as only "saying no." Even well-meaning enforcement can backfire when it lacks context or empathy for operational pressures.

Practical Fix

Start by listening. Where do teams feel stuck? Where have they been burned in the past? Understanding their friction points builds rapport and gives you leverage to shape better solutions.

Reframe your input. Replace "no" with "yes, if…" For example: "Yes, if the retention schedule is followed and consent is captured." This positions privacy as enabling, not obstructing.

Equip, don't just enforce. Offer templates, checklists, and examples that let teams move faster with less risk. Reduce guesswork.

Go where the work happens. Join working sessions, attend standups, offer Slack drop-ins. Visibility changes perception.

Shift from gatekeeper to guide. The goal isn't to control every decision. It's to embed good judgment across the org so privacy doesn't have to be in every room.

Your long-term influence grows when privacy is seen as a helpful, expert partner – not an external auditor.

Leadership Sees Privacy as Pure Overhead

When leadership delays investment, resists headcount, or sees privacy as "just compliance," the issue is rarely that they don't care. It's that privacy has not been translated into business terms they recognize or tied to outcomes they value.

Practical Fix

Speak in outcomes, not obligations. Don't lead with "We have to." Lead with: "This cuts unsubscribe rates by 30%" or "This helps us retain high-value customers in California."

Build a narrative around risk avoided and trust gained. For example: "This prevented a $50K ad tech fine" or "We resolved 98% of DSARs within SLA and no escalations."

Quantify small wins. A smooth intake form, faster vendor onboarding, fewer legal reviews – these add up. Show time and cost saved.

Frame privacy as enablement. Instead of "We can't launch this," try "Here's how to launch it with less regulatory risk and stronger customer retention."

Tell success stories. Not hypotheticals but real ones. Highlight when privacy helped close a deal, kept a customer, or sped up legal review.

Leaders invest in what they understand. Your job is to translate privacy into the metrics, risks, and opportunities they already track.

When Compliance Issues Surface

Missing a Regulatory Requirement

Compliance gaps can emerge from many places: evolving laws, inherited tech debt, decentralized decision-making, or simple human error. Whether it's a missing disclosure, an outdated contract clause, or an overlooked opt-out mechanism, what matters most is how you respond.

Practical Fix

Assess and document the gap, even if only in bullet points for now. Be mindful of privilege: when the issue is sensitive, stick to verbal updates until Legal advises otherwise.

Prioritize by risk and visibility. A broken cookie banner seen by thousands carries more urgency than a buried privacy notice clause.

Implement temporary mitigations. These could include manual processes, interim notices, or holding off on certain data uses while the fix is in progress.

Track the fix through resolution. Create a working log (even informal) that shows actions taken, so you're not starting from scratch if it resurfaces.

Bring in Legal early. Don't wait until there's external exposure. Your role is practical remediation – identifying what went wrong, stopping the bleeding, and stabilizing the process. Let Legal handle privilege, risk analysis, and disclosure strategy.

When Regulators Contact You Directly

Even if it's "just a question," a call or email from a regulator signals scrutiny. These initial contacts are often informal, but how they're handled can influence tone, trust, and trajectory.

Practical Fix

Do not engage directly. Responding, even with a helpful clarification, can open risk or waive privilege.

Forward the communication to Legal within hours, not days. Include the full message, sender information, and any context you have (e.g., related program, recent issue, ongoing audit).

Document what was received and what you did. Keep a simple internal note: who contacted you, when, what was said, and when it was escalated.

Let Legal lead. Your job is to provide accurate, complete background and relevant documentation. Legal owns the strategy and communications.

Be available. Regulators often move quickly once engaged. Stay ready to answer internal questions, pull evidence, or explain processes. Your role is foundational to any credible response.

Handling regulator contact well isn't about legal heroics – it's about speed, clarity, and precision.

When Communication Fails

Nobody Reads Your Privacy Updates

You spend time crafting thoughtful updates but they go unread, filed under "for later," or skimmed and misunderstood. This isn't just a communication issue; it's an influence issue. If privacy messages don't cut through the noise, key guidance gets missed and compliance suffers.

Practical Fix

Reduce frequency, increase precision. A monthly digest that says too much says nothing at all. Shift to need-to-know messages tied to specific changes, decisions, or deadlines.

Use subject lines that create clarity and urgency. Not: *"Privacy Policy Update"* but: *"Consent Settings Changed – Marketing Action by Friday."*

Match the format to the team. Some teams prefer one-pagers; others want a two-minute Loom walkthrough. Ask once, then standardize.

Use embedded calls to action. Link directly to the checklist, policy change, or required action rather than assume they'll read through and find it.

Don't aim for comprehensive. Aim for *relevant and timely.* If it doesn't change what someone needs to do, it probably doesn't belong in the update.

Teams Don't Know When to Involve Privacy

If you're constantly looped in too late or bombarded with low-risk questions, it means your engagement signals aren't clear. Teams don't know when privacy is essential versus optional, or how to route the right questions fast.

Practical Fix

Create intake cues tied to real scenarios. Not just "when using personal data," but: "Involve privacy if collecting emails, tracking behavior, or launching a new vendor."

Provide front-door clarity. A short intake form with routing logic ("new vendor," "new tool," "new data") beats a generic inbox every time.

Hold regular office hours. Offer short weekly or biweekly slots with teams like Marketing, Product, or Legal. These catch issues early and normalize collaboration.

Give teams a way to self-triage. A 1-page "When to Call Privacy" cheat sheet at onboarding, or a Slack pinned post in high-volume channels, can reduce both misses and noise.

Celebrate good timing. Highlight when teams brought privacy in early and saved time or prevented rework. This reinforces the behavior you want.

The goal isn't just more communication. It's better-timed, better-targeted, and more usable communication. That's what builds operational muscle across the organization.

Building Operational Resilience

Resilient programs are not perfect. They are prepared, adaptable, and responsive.

Expect Some Failure

Build redundancy into your processes so that no function is reliant on a single individual or undocumented know-how. Cross-train team members on core tasks, and document critical steps in clear, accessible formats. This prepares your team to absorb disruption without halting operations.

Monitor for Strain

Early signals of stress, such as longer turnaround times, repeated requests for clarification, or a sudden silence from previously engaged teams, should not be ignored. These often point to burnout, disengagement, or unclear expectations.

Stay Nimble

Resist the urge to overengineer workflows. Complex systems are harder to maintain under pressure. Instead, design modular components that can be adjusted as needs evolve. Set calendar reminders to review and refresh operational procedures every quarter.

Follow the 24-Hour Rule

When a process breaks, you don't need to fix everything immediately but you do need to respond fast. Make visible progress within one business day:

- Acknowledge the problem clearly
- Outline short-term actions
- Set expectations for next steps

This approach demonstrates control and reinforces team confidence, even during disruption.

Final Note

Troubleshooting is not just reactive. It's a core competency. The strength of your privacy program lies not in avoiding every mistake but in how well you recover. The ability to diagnose, repair, and adapt when things go wrong builds credibility, earns trust, and lays the groundwork for long-term success.

CHAPTER 19:

FROM CIPP TO CAREER: WHAT COMES NEXT

Mapping Your Privacy Career Path and Deciding What Energizes You

You passed the CIPP. You've built a working privacy program. You've developed some influence and sustained your energy through the challenging early phases of privacy work.

Now what?

This is the question I hear from privacy professionals at various stages of their careers. Whether you're six months into your first privacy role, three years into building programs, or five years in and wondering about your next major move, the same uncertainty emerges: you've proven you can do privacy work, but you're not sure where privacy work can take you.

Here's what I've learned from watching privacy careers develop: there are more diverse paths than you might expect, but the progression is often less clear than traditional career guides suggest. The question isn't whether you have a future in privacy; it's which direction feels right for you and how to navigate the unique challenges of a relatively new field.

The principles in this chapter apply regardless of your current experience level. The specific opportunities available to you will depend on where you are now, but the framework for thinking about your next move remains the same.

The Reality of Privacy Career Progression

Privacy careers don't seem to follow neat hierarchies like accounting or marketing. The field is young enough that many senior privacy professionals built their careers by figuring things out as they went along. This creates both opportunity and uncertainty.

Some privacy leaders came from legal backgrounds and learned business operations. Others started in technology and picked up regulatory knowledge. Many began in other functions and moved into privacy when their organizations needed someone to "figure it out."

This diversity means there's no single path to success, but it also means you need to be more intentional about developing the combination of skills that will take you where you want to go.

Six Paths People Actually Take

From watching career progressions, I've noticed people tend to gravitate toward one of these areas, though many successful careers combine elements from multiple paths.

Privacy Operations: Building Systems That Work

This is the path for people who get energized by making things run smoothly. Privacy operations professionals focus on processing data subject requests, managing vendor assessments, maintaining policies, delivering training, and monitoring compliance.

Career trajectory: A privacy colleague started as a privacy coordinator at a mid-size software company, handling 20-30 data subject requests monthly. She discovered she had a talent for building efficient processes and training people to use them. Within 18 months, she had reduced average DSR response time from 25 days to 8 days and built a vendor assessment process that scaled from 50 to 200 vendors annually. Three years later, she managed privacy operations for a company with 2,000 employees, leading a team of four and managing a $800K annual privacy operations budget.

- **Key skills:** Process optimization, project management, training development, compliance monitoring, vendor management, data analysis
- **Compensation progression:** Generally offers solid mid-market compensation that grows steadily with experience and team management responsibilities
- **Builder vs. Maintainer appeal:** This path appeals to both. Builders enjoy creating new processes and systems from scratch. Maintainers thrive on optimizing existing workflows and achieving operational excellence.

Privacy Technology: Making Tools Work

This path is for people who enjoy the technical side of privacy, whether that's building new solutions, implementing existing tools, or helping organizations use technology to solve privacy challenges.

The vendor ecosystem path: One colleague started in customer success at a consent management platform, helping clients implement and optimize their privacy tools. She discovered she loved understanding both the technical capabilities and the business challenges customers faced. Within three years, she had moved into product management, working directly with engineering teams to build features that customers actually needed. Now she leads product strategy at a privacy automation company, earning significantly more than her previous compliance role while traveling to speak at industry conferences.

The internal implementation path: Another professional started as a privacy analyst but got pulled into evaluating and implementing privacy technology for his company. He became the go-to person for integrating their new data discovery platform with existing systems, then led the rollout of automated DSR processing tools. His technical skills and privacy knowledge made him valuable enough that he now manages privacy technology across multiple business units, with vendors regularly trying to recruit him.

The entrepreneur path: Many former regulatory folks and internal privacy people saw opportunities in the market and had that entrepreneurial spirit. Some had no privacy experience but recognized problems that needed solving. Some have scaled and sold their companies, others love the building process and continue growing their ventures – either way, they're creating the tools that shape how organizations handle privacy.

- **Key skills:** Technical implementation, system integration, vendor evaluation, product management, customer relationship management, or software development, depending on your specific focus
- **Compensation progression:** Wide range depending on role – vendor-side roles often include equity upside, internal roles command premium salaries for technical privacy expertise, and entrepreneurial paths offer unlimited but risky potential
- **Builder vs. Maintainer appeal:** Strong appeal to both. Builders gravitate toward creating new solutions or innovative implementations. Maintainers excel at optimizing existing privacy tech stacks and ensuring reliable system performance.

Privacy Legal and Regulatory: Navigating Complex Requirements

This path focuses on the legal and regulatory aspects of privacy, often requiring deeper legal analysis and closer work with government affairs or legal teams.

Professional development path: A privacy professional I know started as a paralegal at a law firm doing privacy work. She earned her privacy certifications while working on client compliance projects and eventually moved in-house as privacy counsel. She now manages regulatory relationships for a healthcare technology company, handling everything from regulatory submissions to responding to government inquiries and shaping the company's position on emerging privacy legislation.

- **Key skills:** Legal research and analysis, regulatory interpretation, government relations, risk assessment, contract negotiation, policy development
- **Compensation progression:** Offers wide variation depending on legal background and seniority, with senior counsel and CPO roles commanding some of the highest compensation in privacy
- **Builder vs. Maintainer appeal:** Builders enjoy creating new legal frameworks and compliance strategies. Maintainers focus on optimizing existing legal processes and maintaining regulatory relationships.

Privacy Consulting: Solving Diverse Challenges

This path involves providing privacy expertise to multiple organizations, either as an independent consultant or as part of a consulting firm.

Typical evolution: This was my eventual path. After 12+ years building privacy programs at two different companies and leading privacy strategy at a leading privacy tech company, I ventured into consulting, focusing on operational privacy compliance. I enjoy the variety of working with different clients and adapting privacy approaches to diverse organizational cultures.

- **Key skills:** Client relationship management, project management, business development, presentation skills, adaptability, deep domain expertise
- **Compensation progression:** Often offers higher earning potential than in-house roles, especially for senior consultants and partners, but with more variability and less predictable income
- **Builder vs. Maintainer appeal:** Primarily attracts builders who enjoy creating customized solutions for different organizational challenges. It's a great path for natural entrepreneurs. It may be less appealing to maintainers who prefer working within established systems.

Privacy Leadership: Beyond Privacy Roles

This path is about developing executive presence and strategic thinking skills through privacy work, then leveraging those capabilities into broader leadership roles outside of privacy.

Leadership pathway: Privacy often serves as an unexpected executive training ground. One professional started as a hands-on project and legal analyst at a privacy research firm. But privacy work demanded more than technical analysis – she had to navigate organizational politics, influence skeptical stakeholders, and drive change across resistant departments. Her ability to evolve products while managing competing priorities caught leadership's attention. She now leads product development at a senior level, applying the stakeholder management and strategic problem-solving skills she honed in privacy to drive business outcomes.

Another colleague's journey from privacy officer to CPO to broader C-suite roles illustrates how privacy work develops the exact capabilities organizations need in senior executives. Privacy forces you to become fluent in risk, comfortable with ambiguity, and skilled at translating complex requirements into actionable business decisions. These aren't privacy skills – they're leadership skills.

The pattern is clear: privacy work requires you to influence without authority, coordinate across silos that don't naturally collaborate, communicate technical complexity to non-technical audiences, and solve problems that lack clear precedents. Organizations desperately need leaders who can do exactly these things.

- ☞ **Key skills:** Executive influence, stakeholder alignment, risk translation, organizational change management, cross-functional orchestration, strategic problem-solving under uncertainty
- ☞ **Compensation progression:** Offers the highest long-term compensation potential as you transition into broader executive roles with expanded scope, equity participation, and strategic responsibility
- ☞ **Builder vs. Maintainer appeal:** Exclusively attracts builders who thrive on creating organizational capabilities and tackling ambiguous, high-stakes challenges. Maintainers will find this path frustrating and unrewarding.

The AI Governance Pivot: Opportunity or Threat?

Many privacy professionals are asking whether AI governance represents the future of their careers or a threat to their current roles. The reality is more nuanced than either fear suggests.

The landscape shift: Organizations are increasingly tasking privacy professionals with AI governance responsibilities, with many building AI governance programs directly out of their existing privacy functions. A majority of privacy professionals appear to have been tasked with additional responsibilities alongside their existing privacy roles, with AI governance being one of the most common expansions. This isn't happening because AI governance and privacy are the same thing – they're not. It's happening because privacy professionals have already developed the foundational skills that AI governance requires.

Why privacy professionals are natural candidates: The skills that make someone effective at privacy work translate remarkably well to AI governance. You already know how to navigate regulatory ambiguity, translate complex technical requirements into business language, coordinate across resistant organizational silos, and manage risk in rapidly evolving environments. These transferable skills, like stakeholder management, risk assessment, regulatory interpretation, and cross-functional coordination, form the foundation of effective AI governance.

The career reality: Some privacy professionals worry that AI governance will replace privacy work entirely. This misunderstands both fields. I personally don't believe privacy is going anywhere, just yet. AI creates more privacy compliance complexity. What's happening instead is that organizations need people who can manage the intersection between privacy, AI ethics, algorithmic accountability, and emerging AI regulations like the EU AI Act. Privacy professionals who understand this intersection become more valuable, not less.

Three approaches to the transition

1. **The gradual expansion approach:** Many professionals are adding AI governance to their existing privacy responsibilities. Organizations commonly adapt existing privacy structures and processes, such as adding AI-relevant questions to privacy impact assessments. This allows you to build AI governance expertise while maintaining your privacy foundation.

2. **The specialization approach:** Some professionals are pursuing dedicated AI governance certifications like the IAPP's AIGP (Artificial Intelligence Governance Professional) to establish themselves as specialists in this emerging field. This positions you as an expert in AI governance specifically, rather than someone who does privacy plus AI.

3. **The leadership approach:** The most strategic professionals recognize that AI governance isn't just about compliance, it's about helping or-

ganizations navigate one of the most significant technological shifts in decades. These professionals are positioning themselves as strategic advisors who can help leadership teams understand how to deploy AI responsibly while managing business risk.

The skills gap reality

Organizations are reporting that finding qualified AI governance professionals is one of their biggest challenges. This creates a significant opportunity for privacy professionals who can bridge this gap. AI governance roles are growing exponentially, driven by new regulations, corporate accountability demands, and investor pressure for better risk management.

What this means for your career: AI governance isn't a pivot away from privacy, it can be an expansion of what privacy professionals do. The demand for people who understand both privacy and AI governance will only increase as organizations grapple with regulations like the EU AI Act, algorithmic auditing requirements, and the privacy implications of AI systems. Privacy professionals who develop AI governance expertise aren't abandoning their foundation; they're building on it.

- ☞ **Key skills to develop:** AI system lifecycle understanding, algorithmic risk assessment, AI ethics frameworks, emerging AI regulations, cross-functional AI program management
- ☞ **Compensation implications:** AI governance roles typically command premium compensation due to skill scarcity and strategic importance, often 20-40% above equivalent privacy-only roles
- ☞ **Builder vs. Maintainer appeal:** Heavily favors builders who enjoy working in emerging, rapidly evolving fields with ambiguous requirements. Maintainers may find the current lack of standardized frameworks frustrating.

What Actually Matters for Long-Term Success

From watching privacy careers develop over the past decade, a few patterns seem consistently important.

Business understanding often matters more than legal expertise. The privacy professionals who advance most understand how privacy connects to business objectives, not just regulatory requirements. This means being able to explain why a privacy investment will improve customer trust, reduce business risk, or create competitive advantage.

Relationships compound over time. Privacy work depends heavily on relationships, both within your organization and in the broader privacy community. The vendor you assess fairly today might offer you a job in two years. The colleague you help with a difficult DSR might recommend you for a promotion later. I was able to build a consulting practice primarily through referrals from people I had worked with in previous roles.

Specialization creates opportunities. Whether it's a specific industry, a particular technology, or a type of privacy work, developing deep expertise in something specific seems to accelerate career development. Professionals can become the go-to person for privacy in AI systems and later command premium consulting rates because of that specialized knowledge.

Contributing to the community builds reputation. Speaking at conferences, writing about privacy topics, mentoring newer professionals, or participating in privacy organizations appears to accelerate career progression.

Staying current is non-optional. Privacy evolves rapidly, so continuous learning about new laws, emerging technologies, and evolving best practices is essential. This includes formal education, professional development, and staying connected to industry discussions.

A Framework for Your Next Move

Before making any major career decisions, I have learned from my mentors that it is a valuable exercise to spend time understanding what energizes you in your current privacy work and what feels like a chore.

Assess your energy sources: Do you look forward to vendor assessments because you enjoy evaluating systems and processes, or do you dread them because they feel repetitive? When you're working on policy updates, are you energized by translating legal requirements into practical guidance, or frustrated by the ambiguity?

Map your preferences to career paths. Try this framework to identify which direction might fit best:

- High energy from building processes + working with people = Privacy Operations
- High energy from technical problem-solving + creating new systems = Privacy Technology
- High energy from legal analysis + regulatory complexity = Privacy Legal and Regulatory
- High energy from variety + solving different problems = Privacy Consulting
- High energy from strategic thinking + influencing business decisions = Privacy Strategy and Leadership

Research specific roles. Talk to privacy professionals in different types of roles to understand their day-to-day work. Most privacy professionals are generous with their time when talking to people who are genuinely interested in the field. Ask specific questions about what they spend their time on, what challenges they face, and what they find most rewarding.

Consider your options systematically. You might want to stay and grow in your current organization. You might want to move to a different organization that offers better development opportunities. You might shift focus from operational to technical, legal, or consulting work. You might explore international privacy opportunities or apply your privacy skills in different industries.

Building Toward Your Next Role

Start building relationships before you need them. Attend local privacy meetups, join professional organizations like the IAPP, connect with privacy professionals on LinkedIn, and look for opportunities to collaborate with colleagues in other functions.

Develop expertise using the "T-shaped" approach. Build broad competence across privacy fundamentals (the horizontal part of the T) while developing deep expertise in one specific area (the vertical part). This might be based on your organization's industry, the technology you work with, or the type of privacy challenges you find most interesting.

Document your impact and build a portfolio. Keep track of the programs you've built, the processes you've improved, and the problems you've solved. Privacy work is often invisible, so you need to be intentional about capturing and communicating your contributions. Create a simple document tracking projects, outcomes, and business impact.

Stay curious about emerging opportunities. Privacy intersects with artificial intelligence, international business, cybersecurity, product development, and customer experience in ways that create new types of roles. The privacy professional who understands AI governance today will have significant advantages as organizations grapple with AI privacy challenges.

The Reality Check

Your privacy career probably won't follow a linear path. You might start in operations and discover you love the technical aspects. You might plan to stay in-house and end up consulting. You might focus on one industry and find opportunities in a completely different sector.

This unpredictability is actually an advantage! The diversity of privacy career paths means you have flexibility to evolve as you learn more about yourself and as the field continues to develop.

The foundation you've built gives you many options for where to go next. The key is finding the path that matches what energizes you and where you want to make an impact.

Your privacy career is just beginning, and the best part might be that you get to help define what privacy careers look like as the field continues to mature.

CHAPTER 20:

IF I HAD TO START OVER

Strategic Lessons From 20+ Years of Building Privacy Programs That Survive and Scale

After spending 20+ years building or supporting the build of privacy programs, I've learned that most privacy professionals optimize for the wrong things early in their careers.

We tend to optimize for comprehensive coverage when we should optimize for organizational resilience. We optimize for regulatory perfection when we should optimize for business integration. We optimize for individual expertise when we should optimize for institutional capability.

These aren't obvious mistakes. They're strategic blind spots that only become clear after you've built programs that failed, succeeded, and evolved through multiple business cycles.

While I've discussed many of the concepts below in previous chapters, I'd like to highlight them here as we close.

The Three Strategic Mistakes I Made (And See Everywhere)

Mistake 1: Building Programs That Can't Survive Leadership Changes

In my second position in privacy, we built an elegant program around a CEO who genuinely cared about privacy. Detailed policies, sophisticated risk assessments, quarterly board reporting. I thought we were building enterprise-grade privacy.

Then the company got acquired. New leadership saw privacy as compliance overhead. Within six months, our carefully constructed program was dismantled. The policies became shelf-ware. The risk assessments became checkbox exercises. The quarterly reports became annual check-ins.

The lesson: Privacy programs must survive leadership transitions, economic downturns, and strategic pivots. Build for institutional resilience, not executive enthusiasm.

What resilience looks like: Privacy capabilities embedded in business processes rather than dependent on privacy champions. Simple, maintainable processes that function without constant attention. Value creation that's visible to any leadership team, not just privacy-conscious ones.

Mistake 2: Treating Privacy Technology as a Solution Rather Than an Amplifier

During my five years leading global strategy for a privacy tech company, I saw the same pattern repeatedly: organizations buying sophisticated platforms expecting them to solve organizational problems. Data discovery tools purchased to avoid having difficult conversations about data retention. Consent management platforms implemented to avoid training marketing teams about consent requirements.

Technology can accelerate good privacy practices, but it can't create them. I watched companies spend millions on platforms that sat unused because they hadn't built the organizational foundation to support them.

The lesson: Technology amplifies whatever organizational capability you already have. Strong privacy practices become automated and scalable. Weak privacy practices become automated chaos. And without ownership and responsibility, it will fail every time.

What this means practically: Build manual processes that work reliably before automating them. Ensure someone owns privacy outcomes before buying tools to measure them. Create organizational alignment before implementing technology that requires coordination.

Mistake 3: Optimizing for Regulatory Compliance Instead of Business Resilience

Early in my career, I built programs around regulatory requirements. Comprehensive GDPR or CCPA compliance and documentation, detailed international transfer mechanisms. I thought regulatory thoroughness was the goal.

Then I started consulting and saw the programs that actually survived market changes, leadership transitions, and budget cuts. They weren't the most detailed compliant programs. They were the programs that handled regulatory hygiene efficiently without creating business friction.

The lesson: Most privacy work is necessary compliance hygiene. Program sustainability comes from doing this work efficiently and embedding it into business operations rather than treating it as a separate compliance exercise.

What this looks like: Privacy processes that meet regulatory requirements without slowing down business operations. Privacy guidance that helps teams stay compliant while achieving their objectives. Privacy expertise that handles regulatory obligations efficiently, freeing business teams to focus on their core work.

The goal isn't to make privacy a business differentiator. It's to make regulatory compliance as painless and efficient as possible so the business can focus on what actually drives value.

What I'd Build Differently Now

I'd Start with Business Process Integration, Not Policy Development

The most durable privacy programs aren't built around privacy policies. They're built around business processes with embedded privacy controls.

Instead of writing a data retention policy, embed retention decisions into existing business planning cycles. Instead of creating privacy training programs, embed privacy considerations into existing decision-making processes. Instead of building separate privacy workflows, build privacy safeguards into existing operational workflows.

Why this matters: Business processes evolve continuously. Privacy policies get reviewed annually. When privacy is embedded in business processes, it evolves with the business. When privacy is separate from business processes, it becomes outdated and irrelevant.

I'd Build Scaled Human Judgment, Not Automated Compliance

After seeing hundreds of privacy programs, the ones that scale effectively don't eliminate human judgment, they scale it. They create systems that help more people make better privacy decisions rather than trying to automate privacy decisions.

What this looks like: Decision frameworks that help non-privacy professionals assess privacy implications independently. Templates and examples that enable consistent privacy decision-making across teams. Escalation processes that reserve privacy expertise for genuinely complex situations.

The goal isn't reducing privacy work to automated compliance checks. It's building organizational capability to handle privacy considerations at scale.

I'd Optimize for Program Evolution, Not Program Completion

Privacy programs are never finished. Regulations change, technologies evolve, business models shift. The programs that survive aren't usually the most comprehensive ones, they're the most adaptable ones.

What adaptability requires: Modular program components that can be updated independently. Documentation that explains decision-making rationale, not just current requirements. Organizational relationships that survive personnel changes. Processes that can scale up or down based on business needs.

The Strategic Insights That Only Come with Experience

Regulatory Convergence Is Real, But Implementation Varies Dramatically

After working with global privacy requirements for over two decades, I've learned that while privacy laws tend to converge on similar principles, implementation varies dramatically based on organizational culture, industry context, and business model.

What this means: Focus on building capabilities that support privacy principles rather than memorizing specific regulatory requirements. The organizations that adapt fastest to new privacy laws are those with strong foundational capabilities, not those with comprehensive compliance documentation.

Privacy Professionals Scale Through Influence, Not Authority

The privacy professionals who create lasting impact aren't those who accumulate the most authority. They're those who build the most influence across organizational functions.

How influence compounds: Privacy expertise that enables business teams to work efficiently creates advocacy from business leaders. Privacy guidance that prevents problems creates credibility with risk management. Privacy processes that reduce administrative burden create support from operational teams.

This influence becomes your most valuable asset because it survives organizational changes that might eliminate privacy authority.

Global Privacy Approaches Are More Similar Than Different

Working across different regulatory environments taught me that effective privacy programs address the same fundamental challenges regardless of jurisdiction: managing data responsibly, providing transparency about data use, enabling individual control, and preventing harmful data practices.

The strategic implication: Build privacy capabilities that work across regulatory environments rather than building separate programs for different jurisdictions. This creates efficiency and consistency while reducing complexity.

What I'd Tell My Younger Self About Privacy Leadership

Privacy Work Is Change Management, Not Compliance Management

Privacy programs succeed when they help organizations change behavior sustainably. This requires understanding organizational psychology, not just privacy law.

What this means: Spend more time understanding why people resist privacy requirements than learning additional privacy regulations. Build expertise in change management, communication, and organizational development. These skills will serve you throughout your privacy career.

Your Network Is Your Career Development Strategy

Privacy is a relationship-intensive field. The strongest privacy careers are built on networks of relationships across business functions, regulatory environments, and industry sectors.

How to build strategically: Contribute to the privacy community before you need help from it. Build relationships with privacy professionals who are solving different problems than you are. Maintain relationships with former colleagues who move to different organizations or roles. These relationships become sources of opportunities, advice, and support throughout your career.

Specialized Expertise + Broad Business Understanding = Career Acceleration

The privacy professionals who appear to advance fastest develop deep expertise in specific areas while maintaining a broad business perspective.

What this looks like: Deep technical knowledge about privacy engineering combined with understanding of product development processes. Sophisticated regulatory expertise combined with appreciation for business strategy. Advanced vendor risk assessment capabilities combined with understanding of procurement dynamics.

For the Privacy Professional Starting Today

You're entering privacy at a dynamic inflection point. The regulatory environment continues expanding with new state laws, international frameworks, and AI-specific requirements. Technology is making some privacy operations more efficient, but it's also creating new categories of risk that require privacy oversight. Organizations are asking privacy professionals to handle an ever-widening scope of data-related issues.

The opportunities are real: Privacy expertise is becoming essential infrastructure in regulated organizations. Yes, the role is expanding beyond traditional privacy work into AI ethics, data governance, and vendor risk management, but this expansion also creates career opportunities and makes privacy professionals more valuable to organizations.

What this means for your career: You're building skills that will be increasingly in demand. The ability to handle interconnected data issues efficiently makes you indispensable. Learning to manage scope creep strategically, knowing when to expand your expertise and when to maintain boundaries, becomes a core professional competency.

The foundation you build now will determine your options later. Focus on building efficient processes that scale, develop organizational influence that helps you navigate expanding responsibilities, and create capabilities that work across the growing landscape of data-related compliance requirements. You're learning to be adaptable, which is exactly what the field needs.

You're not just building a privacy program. You're building professional capabilities that will help you thrive in whatever new compliance challenges emerge in the rapidly evolving landscape of data regulation.

The work you're doing matters. The field needs thoughtful professionals who can handle expanding responsibilities efficiently and sustainably. You're exactly the kind of person who will shape how privacy work evolves as the field continues to mature.

CHAPTER 21:

BEFORE YOU GO

A Reflection and Invitation to Keep Building Together

This book is about the practical reality of privacy work: mapping data activities, handling business requests, building sustainable processes, tracking progress, building influence, and managing the inevitable scope creep that comes with privacy roles.

But more than that, it's about the experience of doing this work in real organizations with real constraints and real people.

This isn't really an ending. It's a reflection.

What You May Be Building

Take a moment to recognize what you might be working toward:

You may be moving from theory to practice. Moving beyond just knowing privacy law to applying privacy expertise to real business situations. Learning to handle data subject requests, review vendor relationships, guide business decisions, and communicate privacy requirements to stakeholders who think in business terms.

You might be building something sustainable. Creating processes, documentation, and relationships that aren't just compliance theater but working systems that function day-to-day, that other people can use, and that keep working without constant management.

You could be developing professional judgment. Learning to assess privacy risks in ambiguous situations, balance competing priorities, and make practical decisions when there's no clear "right" answer. Finding ways to work within business constraints rather than defaulting to prohibition.

You may be finding your professional voice. Developing the ability to explain privacy concepts clearly, advocate for necessary privacy work, and build support for privacy initiatives. Learning to translate privacy expertise into language that resonates with different audiences.

This progression matters. Many people acquire privacy knowledge through various paths but struggle to translate that expertise into real-world organizational value. Building that bridge between privacy theory and business reality is significant work.

The Emotional Reality of This Work

As noted earlier, privacy work can be emotionally demanding in ways that aren't always obvious.

You carry the weight of protecting people's personal information, often for people who don't even know you exist. You make decisions that affect real individuals' privacy, sometimes with incomplete information and under time pressure. You advocate for privacy protections in organizations that may not naturally prioritize them.

Some days you feel like you're building something meaningful. Other days you feel like you're just checking compliance boxes. Both feelings are valid, and both are part of the work.

The isolation is real. You're often the only person in meetings who's thinking about privacy implications. You're the one asking uncomfortable questions about data use. You're the one who has to say "we need to consider privacy" when everyone else wants to move fast.

But you're also the one who prevents problems before they happen. You're the one who helps people understand what responsible data handling looks like. You're the one who creates systems that work for both privacy protection and business objectives.

The Community You're a Part of

There's a community of thoughtful, experienced professionals working on similar challenges who understand exactly what you're going through.

We're all figuring this out as we go. Privacy is still a relatively young field. The challenges you're facing on an ongoing basis, scope creep, resource constraints, unclear requirements, evolving regulations, are challenges we're all navigating together.

The field needs people who can build programs that work in the real world, not just in theory. You have opportunities to shape what privacy careers look like and how privacy professionals support each other.

A Final Thought

I wrote this for the people doing the work, often figuring it out as they go. For those of you managing consent fatigue, vendor chaos, and impossible timelines while everyone asks "Are we compliant yet?"

You're not behind. None of us are. We're all just building this plane while flying it, learning from each other's mistakes and wins.

> If something here sparked an idea, great. If you think I got something completely wrong, even better, tell me why. The best insights come from the people actually wrestling with these problems every day.
>
> And if reading this just made you feel like someone else gets how hard this work really is, that's probably what matters most. We're all in this together, making it up as we go, trying to build something that actually works.

The work you're doing matters. Not because it's glamorous or because it always feels rewarding, but because it's necessary. Someone has to think about privacy implications. Someone has to ask the hard questions. Someone has to build systems that protect people's information.

You're that someone. And you're doing it well.

What did I miss? What would you do differently? The conversation is just getting started.

Let's Stay in Conversation

Join our newsletter – Regular field notes, practical tools, and behind-the-scenes glimpses from privacy work that holds. Join here: https://blueskyprivacystack.com/

Explore BlueSky PrivacyStack™ – Ready to go deeper? Check out the full kit of templates, trainings, and operational tools here: www.blueskyprivacystack.com

Say hello on LinkedIn – I'd love to hear what resonated – or what you're building. https://www.linkedin.com/in/ttfalk/

Here's to privacy work that holds. And to the people doing it.

Keep going. And keep in touch.

– Teresa (T) Troester-Falk

TOOLKIT INDEX

Throughout this book, you'll find practical examples, frameworks, and starting points that you can adapt to your specific situation. Think of these as the scaffolding for building your own privacy tools, not finished products to copy exactly.

Operational Examples

What You'll Find	How It Helps	Chapter Reference
Sample Data Request Form	See what fields actually matter for processing requests	Chapter 6: Build a Practical DSR Process
DSR Acknowledgment Example	Adapt professional response language for your organization	Chapter 6: Build a Practical DSR Process
DSR Tracking Framework	Build your own system for monitoring request progress	Chapter 6: Build a Practical DSR Process
Data Location Mapping Guide	Structure your search for where personal data actually lives	Chapter 6: Build a Practical DSR Process

What You'll Find	How It Helps	Chapter Reference
Privacy Work Log Approach	Track your activities in ways that demonstrate competence	Chapter 9: Monitoring and Metrics

Assessment Approaches

What You'll Find	How It Helps	Chapter Reference
Activity Mapping Examples	Two different ways to document data flows that people actually use	Chapter 4: Start Here: Map Activities, Not Data
Vendor Risk Triage Method	Prioritize your vendor reviews based on actual risk levels	Chapter 7: Vendors: The "Crawl" Approach
Vendor Review Questions	Focus your assessments on what matters most	Chapter 7: Vendors: The "Crawl" Approach
Vendor Tracking Framework	Organize ongoing vendor oversight without losing track	Chapter 7: Vendors: The "Crawl" Approach

Response Frameworks & Examples

What You'll Find	How It Helps	Chapter Reference
"Yes, If..." Response Methods	Turn privacy roadblocks into collaborative solutions	Chapter 8: Handling Business Requests
Common Scenario Examples	See how to handle real requests from marketing, sales, and product teams	Chapter 8: Handling Business Requests

Program Structure

What You'll Find	How It Helps	Chapter Reference
One-Page Program Description	Explain your privacy approach clearly to anyone who asks	Chapter 12: The Minimum Viable Privacy Program

APPENDIX:

PREVIEW OF THE BLUESKY COREFRAME™

When You're Ready to Scale Beyond the Basics

If you've worked through this book, you've built something real. You're handling data subject requests, reviewing vendors, guiding business decisions, and tracking your progress. You've moved from theoretical privacy knowledge to operational privacy capability.

That's exactly where most privacy professionals need to be.

But as your program matures, different questions emerge: How do you explain what your privacy program actually covers? How do you maintain progress without starting from scratch every quarter? How do you demonstrate systematic privacy management when auditors, executives, or regulators ask?

This is when you need structure that scales, not theoretical frameworks, but practical organization that builds on what you've already created.

What Comes After the Minimum Viable Privacy Program

The work you've been doing through this book naturally falls into eleven operational areas that every mature privacy program needs to address:

1. **Program Ownership & Accountability**
2. **Data Processing Activities**
3. **Data Use, Access & Retention**
4. **Privacy Notice & Transparency**
5. **Consent & Cookie Management**
6. **Privacy Rights & Request Handling**
7. **Vendor & Third-Party Risk Management**
8. **Training, Communication & Culture**
9. **Monitoring, Records & Reporting**
10. **Privacy Impact Assessments**
11. **AI & Automated Decision-Making Governance**

You're probably already working in most of these areas. The CoreFrame simply organizes this work into a structure you can explain, maintain, and defend over time.

Why Structure Matters

Structure isn't about adding complexity. It's about making your existing work more sustainable and defensible.

Consistency across growth. As your organization changes by adding new products, new markets, and new team members, having clear categories helps maintain privacy standards without rebuilding processes from scratch.

Communication with stakeholders. When executives ask about privacy coverage or auditors want to understand your approach, organized structure makes these conversations much easier.

Resource allocation. Clear categories help you identify gaps, prioritize improvements, and justify privacy investments based on comprehensive program coverage.

Professional development. Understanding how your daily privacy work fits into broader program categories helps you see career development opportunities and build more sophisticated privacy expertise.

Building Toward Comprehensive Coverage

The CoreFrame represents the natural evolution of the practical work you've been building. It's not a replacement for the approaches in this book; it's how you organize those approaches into something larger.

Start where you are. Keep doing the practical work that's generating results. When you're ready to add structure that helps you scale, defend, and communicate your privacy program more effectively, the framework will be there.

You're not behind. You're exactly where you need to be, building the foundation that makes everything else possible.

www.ingramcontent.com/pod-product-compliance
Lightning Source LLC
La Vergne TN
LVHW022200200926
848481LV00006B/1797